VICTIMS OF
FOUL PLAY

A TRUE STORY OF
ONE MAN'S DARK SECRETS

PATRICIA LUBECK

Dedication

This book was written in memory of Martha and Jean Larson, two women once married to Clarence Larson, a man with many dark secrets. We may not know all the details of their passing, but their lives were precious, and they were loved. It is my hope that one day, the missing pieces of their stories will be known. Truth and justice will prevail.

TABLE OF CONTENTS

INTRODUCTION

THIS STORY TAKES place in rural Minnesota in Lyon County. The county was established by two acts of the Minnesota state legislature, dated March 6, 1868 and March 2, 1869. The county seat was designated as Marshall. The county was named for Nathaniel Lyon, an Army officer who served in the Dakota and Minnesota territories before being killed in the Civil War in 1861. He had achieved the rank of general by his death. The county was much larger until an act passed on March 6, 1873, made the western 43% the new Lincoln County.

The Yellow Medicine River flows northeast through the upper portion of the county, the Redwood River flows northeast through the central part, and the Cottonwood River flows northeast through the lower part. The county's terrain consists of low rolling hills, etched by gullies. The county has a total of 722 square miles, of which 715 square miles is land

and 7.1 square miles is water.

The first part of this story takes place near the small town of Garvin. The town was originally called Terry, for Union general Alfred Terry, and was platted in 1886 by the railroad. The present name of Garvin was adopted in 1881 for H.C. Garvin, a railroad official.

The town of Tracy is where the rest of the story takes place. Tracy was platted in 1875. It was named for John F. Tracy, another railroad official. The post office has been in operation since 1877. The city was incorporated in 1893.

On June 13, 1968, Tracy was hit by an F5 tornado, which killed nine people and injured 150. Until the 1960s, Tracy was a highly active railroad town on the Chicago & Northwestern Railway as a concentration point for numerous branch lines in the area serving heavy agriculture. Today, Tracy holds an annual summer festival called "Boxcar Days," which takes place over Labor Day weekend, as a sign of the railroad's influence on the town. Currently, Tracy is still a division point on the Canadian Pacific Railway (formerly the Dakota, Minnesota and Eastern Railroad) where railroad crews from both east and west exchange trains.

One of the first settlers in Tracy was John L. Craig. He and his family came to the area and homesteaded 160 acres in October 1878, located on the southeast quarter of section 14, Monroe Township, adjoining the city of Tracy.

Craig was born in Eymouth, Scotland on January 10, 1836. In 1854 he came to the United States and settled in Waukesha County, Wisconsin where he farmed for US Senator I.P. Walker. In Palmyra, Wisconsin, on August 12, 1858, Mr. Craig married Jeffery Craig (maiden name unknown). There were eight children: Oliver, John, Douglas,

Arthur, Carrie, Cora and Jennie, but one child, Lillie died at a young age.

Craig enlisted in the Civil War in 1864. He was taken prisoner at the battle of Guntown, Mississippi and was confined in prison until the close of the war. After the war, he made his way west to the Tracy area. In the fall of 1872, the railroad was built. Until 1875 there was no station; the trains stopped a mile east of the present townsite, at a place called Shetek Crossing. In 1875 and for a year after, trains used the warehouse of Neil Currie for a station, and Mr. Craig was the first station agent.

Craig started the first livery stable in Tracy, in 1877. Before the railroads entered Pipestone, Mr. Craig had the contract for carrying the mail from Tracy to Flandreau, South Dakota. His son John made the trips, and a relief team was kept at Haycock Prairie near Pipestone. After running the livery stable for a few years, Mr. Craig sold out and took up farm work. He had always made his home on the farm even when he was at work in the village. Craig was a charter member of Joe Hooker Post No. 15, G.A.R. and one of its early commanders. "Craig Avenue" in Tracy was named in his honor.

In 1882, John's son Oliver and his wife Lucinda built a beautiful Victorian mansion on five acres of the original homestead on Craig Avenue. A descendant of Oliver, Dr. Jay Craig, and his wife Olga once owned the mansion. He was a well-known veterinarian in Tracy during the 1900s.

Photo of Craig house, circa 1880s
(photo from Rosemary Martin, Tracy, MN)

FAMILY'S EARLY
BEGINNINGS

YOU ARE ABOUT to read the true story of a man named
Clarence Ledu Larson, who kept many dark secrets hidden
until now. First, it's important to start out with the family's
early beginnings. Clarence's grandfather, Lars Ostenson, was
a Norwegian farmer, born in Hamar, Norway in 1826. He
married Emjor Sjurson Vangen and they had two sons—
Kjostel, born 1851, and Austin, born 1856.

Lars was thirty-three years old when he and his two sons
immigrated from Norway in 1859. It was not clear if Emjor
made the trip at this time or if she made the journey later.
The family settled near Decorah, Iowa. Kjostel attended
Luther College and became a pastor, preaching at various
churches in Minnesota, Wisconsin, Iowa and South Dakota.

Sometime before 1871, Lars became a widower. On
January 19, 1871, at the age of forty-five, Lars married

Ronnaug (or Ranad) Knutsdotter, who was twenty years old. Their first son, Carl (aka Charley), was born on February 28, 1873 in Winneshiek County, near Decorah, Iowa.

In researching baptismal records, it was discovered that many of Carl's siblings had the last name of "Ostenson," but by 1900, the census records indicated the family used the last name of "Guttebo." There were five more "Guttebo" children listed: Martin, Christine, Peter, Laura, and Rudolph. It appeared that Carl and his half-brother Austin were the only two who kept the surname of "Larson," but we are not sure why this happened. Carl eventually traveled to Minnesota and made his home in Murray County. Later Christine and her mother Ronnaug moved to Minnesota. Peter, Martin, and Rudolph remained in Iowa. Laura married and settled in Texas.

Lars Ostenson died in 1917 at the age of ninety-one. After the death of her husband, Ronnaug moved in with a son in Decorah, Iowa. Then, around 1925, Ronnaug moved in with her daughter, Christine Aspelin, who lived near Slayton, Murray County. Ronnaug died on August 20, 1939 of heart disease. She was eighty-eight years old. She was taken back to Iowa and buried in Washington Prairie Lutheran Cemetery, Winneshiek County, next to her husband, Lars.

Carl lived with the family until he was a young man, then went to St. Paul, where he eventually met a young woman by the name of Ida Bergetta Enerhaug (aka Anerhaug). Ida was born in Bergen Norway on July 23, 1871. She was raised and educated there and at the age of eighteen, came to America to the home of Professor and Mrs. Whitney of Fairbault—friends who had come to America several years earlier. She was united in marriage to Carl Larson on June 30, 1893 in

St. Paul. The following year, the married couple moved to Murray County. The 1895 census has Carl and Ida living on a farm in Shetek. Carl's occupation was listed as "farmer," and Ida as "housekeeper."

Carl and Ida had six children: James, Roy, Clara, Martha, Nora, and Clarence. The family prospered and by 1905, they had enough money to purchase a 160-acre farm in Skandia Township. Then in the 1930 census, Ida was listed as "married and head of household," living with her son, Roy, on the farm. It appears that Carl may not have been living with the family in 1930 and was not listed in the 1940 census either. He may have left the area to find employment, as the depression hit in 1929 and through the 1930s. Also, the Dust Bowl hit the plains in 1931 and lasted eight years, so times were tough, and many people moved out of the area to find employment.

Ida struggled with life on the farm during this time. She passed away at the Tyler Hospital on the evening of May 19, 1939. Ida had suffered about a week with pneumonia, which caused her death. She was sixty-seven years old. Funeral services were held in the English Lutheran Church of Skandia with Rev. S.A. Stenseth officiating. Interment was in the cemetery beside the church.

Carl passed away at the home of his daughter, Mrs. George Anderson, after a lingering illness. He suffered from diabetes. He died on August 10, 1955 at the age of eighty-two. Funeral services were held at the home of Mrs. George Anderson and at the Skandia Zion Lutheran Church six miles south of Balaton. Pall bearers were all nephews: John, Rudolph and Clair Aspelin, John Dyshan, Levi Guttebo and Leonard Larson. Survivors were his wife, Mary (his second wife), three sons, three daughters, nineteen grandchildren, six great-grandchildren, and a number of other relatives.

From 1940 onward, property records show that there were three farms in the Larson family, owned by brothers James, Roy, and Clarence, all near the Garvin/Skandia area, Murray County.

CLARENCE MARRIES MARTHA

CLARENCE LEDU LARSON was 5'11," 225 pounds with blue eyes and brown hair. He married Martha Hatton on November 30, 1928. They lived on the same farm as Clarence's mother Ida and brother Roy, but apparently in a second smaller house on the property. Clarence and Martha kept busy with life on the big farm. Everyone got along, and Clarence enjoyed spending time with his mother and brother, who were great neighbors.

It was ten years before Clarence and Martha had their first child, Ronald Clarence, born on July 15, 1938 in Tyler. By 1940, Clarence and Martha decided it was time they had their very own farm. They saved enough money to purchase a 124-acre farm in Lake Sarah Township. The farm was located southwest of the Valhalla Corner near Garvin. The small house, which would more accurately be called a shack, was a square structure, about 16' x 16' with a 10' addition built on one end of the house. The interior was one big open space. They had indoor plumbing; the toilet was in the basement. The second floor was another open area where everyone slept in their own bed. They had a hired-hand, Gilly Pearsoll, who lived with the family. Times were tough, but they managed to make things work. Their second child, Janet Lee, was born on August 12, 1943 in Slayton.

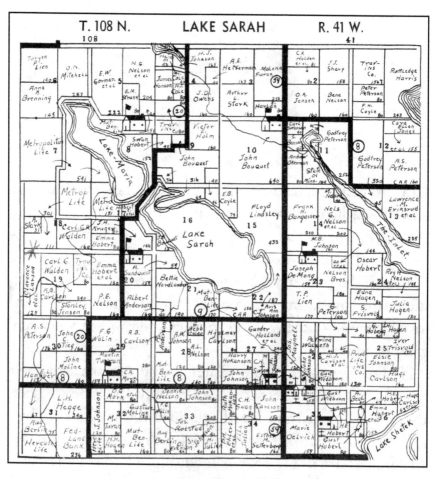

Larson property by asterisk
From platt map on internet

VICTIMS OF FOUL PLAY

Clarence was not much of a farmer; he left everything to Martha and Gilly. Martha had a very hard life. The family lived in a small home, the walls were dark and dingy; the furniture was old, musty, and broken-down; laundry was hung out on a line in good weather, and hung on lines in the basement during the winter. Martha was a very sweet, soft spoken, hard-working woman. She was of average height, about 5'5" to 5'6," a bit on the stocky side. She did what she could to make a nice home for her family. Martha kept a tidy house, took care of the children, made delicious meals and baked goods. Her outside activities included raising hogs and chickens, milking cows, tending a huge garden, canning vegetables, and helping Gilly with the field work. Most of the time Clarence was nowhere around. He was often seen in town, all dressed up, talking with the locals. It was said that he spent time at the Peavey Elevator in Garvin, reading books about true crime.

A terrible event occurred at the Larson farm on June 8, 1955. It was reported in the *Tracy Area Headlight Herald* on June 9. "A fire of undetermined origin destroyed a large barn around 2 a.m. The barn was consumed by flames before Balaton and Tracy firemen arrived. The loss included several hundred bales of hay, along with some corn and flax stored within the barn. No livestock was lost. The Balaton fire department protected surrounding buildings with a water spray so that the fire did not spread. A tractor was pulled away so that the tile wall of the barn would not fall on it. Enroute to the Larson farm, the Tracy fire truck broke down two miles southwest of Garvin, but passing motorists took the men to the fire where they assisted the Balaton department. A wrecker towed the fire truck back to Tracy later that morning. The damage was a broken drive shaft. Sometime in 1945, another barn burned down at the same site as this fire on the Larson farm." I checked for a story about this fire in the local newspapers, but nothing was reported.

By December 1961, Clarence and Martha decided to sell the farm and move to Marshall, where Martha worked at the Swift and Produce Company. They were having some financial difficulties. The children were grown, the couple was getting up in years, and they'd had enough of the busy farm life.

December was a busy time for the Larsons. Clarence realized it would be a huge undertaking to move from the farmhouse into a small place in Marshall, but it would be closer to Martha's employment. He had lots of farm equipment in the outbuildings that would have to be sold or given away to neighbors, just to get rid of it. Martha was busy packing and going through all the household items they had accumulated over the twenty-one years they lived on the farm, and it was a daunting task. She knew she had to part with things to make the move easier, but it was hard, as she was sentimental, and everything she touched had a precious memory that went along with it, especially the little mementoes the children made in school for every holiday.

It was a cold, cloudy day on December 18. Martha sat at the kitchen table writing out Christmas cards, feeling the warmth from the old kitchen stove. She spent some time writing a personal note to Clara Johnson, Clarence's sister, who lived in Tucson, Arizona. Once she finished addressing the envelope, she placed it in a bundle along with the rest

VICTIMS OF FOUL PLAY

of the cards and put them in a box near the front door to be dropped off at the post office the following morning on her way to work. Martha had not gone to work that day, but instead, stayed home so she could pack and sort through the household items.

Martha was exhausted and by 9:30 that evening, she told Clarence she was going upstairs to bed. It seemed the couple slept in separate bedrooms. Martha slept on the second floor and Clarence slept on the main floor.

THE ACCIDENT

THE FOLLOWING MORNING, December 19, the temperature hovered at 15 degrees with some gusty winds. There was six inches of snow on the ground. Clarence awoke at 4:40 a.m. He couldn't sleep so got up, dressed, donned his coat, and went out to the garage to check on the tires of his car. Before he left the house, he heard the clock alarm go off upstairs where Martha slept. She was up by 5:00 a.m. to get ready for work.

After finding the tires on the car in order, he started the 1948 A.M. Farmall tractor and left it running, but before he returned to the house, he shut off the engine of the car. When he entered the house, Martha was standing at the mirror in the kitchen, fixing her hair. She asked, "What is all the noise about outside?" Clarence said, "I started the tractor and I'm going to elevate the corn." Martha expressed a desire to help him since she was concerned about a ruptured disc in his back and commented that he might be crippled up all winter if he did it alone.

Clarence went outside and backed up the tractor to the elevator but found the mechanism frozen before he hooked it up. He made three trips to the basement to fill a five-gallon container with hot water to thaw out the elevator. Clarence had a bad back, so this task might have been difficult, since a five-gallon container filled with water can weigh up to 41 pounds. The house had an outside entrance to the basement and the distance was about 125 feet, so it would take quite a bit of time to haul water back and forth to the elevator. After the elevator was thawed, he returned to the house for a dry pair of gloves. Martha was at the piano playing a hymn. She was wearing a storm coat over her slacks, but under her slacks, she still wore her pajama bottoms, to stay a bit warmer.

Clarence told her the machinery was ready to go, and she came outside shortly thereafter to help him. He increased the speed of the tractor a little bit and she began shoveling in corn on the right side of the elevator and he on the left.

After they had nearly completed the job, with only a little cleaning up to do, Clarence climbed the ladder to the top of the crib to level off the corn with a four-tine straw fork. He had just put the fork to his shoulder and started clawing the corn when everything stopped dead. He looked down and saw Martha's feet and legs sticking out from the power take-off.

Getting down from the ladder as fast as he could, he ran around the power take-off shaft and felt for her pulse on her throat and arm but couldn't find any signs of life. Her eyes were wide open and staring off to the left. Clarence saw and heard blood running out of the back of her head, running straight down into the wet snow.

Clarence ran to the house, called Dr. Remsberg of Tracy, followed by a call to his neighbor, Arvid Anderson. Then he rushed back to the elevator to check on Martha but could not feel a pulse; poor Martha was dead.

The neighbors, Arvid and Rueben Anderson, were the first on the scene. The doctor arrived shortly after the tragedy occurred and determined the woman had been killed almost instantly. M.C. Ohman and Vernon Butson arrived by ambulance from Tracy sometime later and transported the body to Swenson's Mortuary in Balaton.

It was not until after the body had arrived at the mortuary and embalming processes begun that the Murray County Coroner, Dr. Hugh Patterson of Slayton was notified of the death. He arrived a brief time later, examined the body and noticed a large gash on the back of the skull. At that time, the doctor immediately stopped the mortician from proceeding with the embalming process.

Dr. Patterson contacted Sheriff Neumann of Tracy to investigate the suspicious death. Because of the nature of the death, it was determined that the autopsy should be performed by Dr. John W. Alexander, a highly experienced pathologist. The body was transported to Sioux Falls, South Dakota where Dr. Alexander performed the autopsy on December 20, 1961. In his opinion, Martha Larson died of head injuries and that the other injuries on her body were sustained after death. The lack of bleeding by bone fragments from the ribs penetrating the chest cavity would be related to a postmortem injury. There was no brain damage to the front of the brain.

An inquest was scheduled the day after Martha's death by

Dr. Hugh Patterson, but he recessed it until August 1962. It was advised that law enforcement and other officials conduct a thorough investigation into the suspicious death.

Martha Larson
(photo from Larry Sloan collection)

Funeral services for Martha Larson were held on Friday, December 21, at the Zion Lutheran Church just south of Balaton. Interment was in the church cemetery. Rev. Bennert Solberg of Garvin and Rev. Daniel Jordahl of Marshall conducted the service.

Martha M. Hatton was born at Lowell, Indiana on May 13, 1909, the daughter of Francis and Alvora. In 1918 she and her family moved to the Balaton community, where she spent most of her life until her marriage to Clarence L. Larson on November 30, 1928. She was survived by her husband Clarence and two children, Ronald of Marshall and Janet of Sioux Falls, along with her mother Alvora Hatton of Garvin. Other survivors were three brothers, Herman, Charles, and Clair; one sister, Mrs. Alfred Nelson; two grandchildren, and other relatives and friends. Pallbearers were Rueben Anderson, William Pearson, Raymond Swift, Rudy Aspelin, Paul Erickson, and John Engesser.

RECONVENING OF
THE INQUEST

BECAUSE OF THE suspicious nature of Martha's death, a second autopsy was performed by Dr. John Coe, pathologist at the Minneapolis General Hospital. Martha's body was exhumed in April 1962. After Dr. Coe's extensive examination, Martha's remains were re-interred at the Zion Lutheran Church cemetery.

A Murray County coroner's jury composed of six men and two women heard evidence concerning the death of Martha Larson on August 14, 1962 at the courthouse in Slayton. This matter was held at the request of J. T. Schueller, County Attorney for the County of Murray, Fulda, Minnesota, by Henry Feikema, Special Assistant Attorney General, for Attorney General Walter F. Mondale, and Dr. Hugh Patterson, presiding before a coroner's jury. Dr. Patterson stated to the jury that this was a reconvening of the adjourned coroner's inquest held at the Murray

County Memorial Hospital on December 20, 1961 in the presence of the body of Martha Larson.

Special Assistant Attorney General Henry Feikema called Clarence Larson as the first witness on the stand to describe the circumstances leading to Martha's death.

Clarence stated he arose at about 4:40 a.m. and went out to check the tires on the car. He started the car and left it running and then started the tractor. He left the tractor running but turned off the car before entering the house. Martha was up and in her bathrobe. She said, "We better elevate that corn this morning before I go to work." And I said, "I could elevate it later that day and she said, "We better elevate it now while the tractor is going. I will help you put that corn up." So, then I went out and backed the tractor out of the garage, over to the elevator, and the elevator was frozen. There was only about 20 bushels of corn on the ground that had to be elevated. The base of the elevator was frozen from snow collecting in it, so I got a five-gallon can out of the garage and went down in the basement and got hot water out of the hot water heater and it took three cans to thaw it out. It took about twenty minutes to thaw it out. Then I took the shaft that fits on the elevator and turned it by hand to be sure that all the ice was out, and started it up so she didn't start up at high speed and break the shaft. Then I hooked the thing to the power take off—hooked the power take-off shaft onto the tractor and let it run slow. Then I went in the house to get some dry mitts and Martha was sitting at the piano. She said, "Have you got the elevator going?" And I said, "Yes I have." "I am dressed warm so I will come out and help you," she said. The time was about 5:30 am.

Feikema asked the following key questions relating to Martha and the farm equipment, along with more detailed questions about how the accident occurred.

Q. *What kind of a tractor was this?*
A. *A.M. Farmall.*
Q. *And what year was it?*
A. *'48.*
Q. *This tractor had a power take-off attachment that you used with it, is that correct?*
A. *Yes.*
Q. *And it also had a tow bar on the back, is that correct?*
A. *Yes.*
Q. *I wonder if you could describe the kind of tow bar that was on the back of this tractor.*
A. *It was attached underneath the tractor and was mounted on the back of the main drawbar so that it could swing if you pulled the pins out. That is for farm work.*
Q. *So then there was a permanent bar back there, is that correct?*
A. *Yes.*
Q. *Is this a photograph of the drawbar that you have described?*
A. *Yes.*
Q. *How long had you lived on the farm?*
A. *Since the spring of 1940.*
Q. *In addition to your wife working as a housewife on the farm, she was employed outside of the home as well, wasn't she?*
A. *Yes.*
Q. *And she worked in Marshall, is that correct?*

A. Yes, at the produce plant.

Q. She hadn't worked on Monday, is that right?

A. No, that is right.

Q. Had she been feeling all right on Monday?

A. Yes.

Q. So she came out to help you, is that right?

A. Yes.

Q. That was about five-thirty then?

A. About that, maybe a little bit before.

Q. So what did you do then?

A. Well, we went out and started to elevate the corn.

Q. Do you have a yard light out there?

A. Yes.

Q. Was the yard light on?

A. I thought I had it on, but I had the light on my tractor and there is one big light on the back.

Q. How many lights in back, one?

A. Yes, and two in front.

Q. When you first went out there that morning did you turn the light on to make your way over to the garage?

A. Yes.

Q. And you turned the light on from the kitchen, is that right?

A. Yes.

Q. And did you turn it off at any time while you were out there?

A. No, I didn't turn off the light.

Q. And it wasn't turned off while you were out there, was it?

A. No.

Q. So the two of you went out there and started to elevate the corn, is that right?

A. Yes.

Q. And would the yard light shed light on the area in which you were working?

A. Yes, it would.

Q. So then both of you started to elevate the corn?

A. Yes.

Q. Then what happened?

A. We finished up shoveling the pile and there was a little to clean up and Martha was cleaning up around and I walked up around the front of the tractor, up to the crib to see how the corn was stacking up under the elevator.

Q. How long did it take to elevate 20 bushels?

A. Not very long, maybe ten minutes.

Q. So you went up to check the corn to see how it was levelling out up there?

A. Yes.

Q. Then what happened?

A. I just got ahold of my fork to rake the corn over and I heard the tractor just make kind of a growling stop. Then I looked down and I could see Martha's foot sticking out from back of the edge of the tire and the tractor stopped completely.

Q. Had the tractor shut off, did it stall?

A. It stalled.

Q. It was no longer running?

A. It was no longer running. It just made kind of a r-o-w-r-r.

Q. What were you using to get the corn into the elevator?

A. Scoop shovels.

Q. You didn't hear a scoop shovel drop or hit the elevator or anything?

A. No.

Q. What did you do when you got down off the crib?

A. I came around the front of the tractor and came in back of the tractor where she was.

Q. Can you tell me why you went all the way around the tractor, rather than coming from the ladder straight over from the elevator?

A. Well, that was almost in line with the crib, when I got down, I just ran around like this (indicating).

Q. Now describe the position that you found her in when you came around the tractor? Describe where her feet were, where the body was and the rest of it.

A. Well she was on the east side of the drawbar, the power take-off. Her right arm was twisted around the power take off shaft and her head was back underneath the tractor like this (indicating).

Q. The right arm was around the drawbar?

A. Around the power take-off.

Q. No, no, just this (indicating).

A. This piece—

Q. From here to here (indicating).

A. That is the slip clutch.

Q. Her arm was wrapped around the clutch, is that correct?

A. Yes.

Q. Where was the rest of her body with respect to this? Just straight along parallel with the power take-off shaft?

A. Yes.

Q. And her legs, were they entangled at all?

A. No.

Q. At the time you found her in this position, was she

then alive?

A. No.

Q. How did you determine this?

A. I felt for a pulse in her arm and I didn't get any pulse and there wasn't any pulse in her throat and the blood was running in a stream almost as big as your little finger out the back of her head.

Q. Was there any blood from any other area?

A. Not that I noticed.

Q. To the best of your knowledge, you didn't hear her fall into the tractor, is that correct?

A. No I didn't.

Q. She made no outcry whatsoever?

A. No.

Q. You only heard one sound and that was the noise from the tractor stopping, is that correct?

A. That is right.

Q. What was the first thing you did after you felt the pulse?

A. I ran in and called Dr. Remsberg.

Q. Where was he?

A. At Tracy, Minnesota.

Q. How far is Tracy from here?

A. About 13 miles.

Q. How far is Slayton from there?

A. About the same distance.

Q. Did you remove Martha from the position in which she was caught?

A. No, I didn't.

Q. Did you turn the switch off on the tractor?

A. There is no switch on it. It is a magneto type.

Q. Is there a way of disengaging this power take-off on

the back of it?

A. Yes.

Q. *There is a lever there. Isn't that correct?*

A. *It is a rod.*

Q. *Was that pushed down at the time you came around there?*

A. *That I don't remember.*

Q. *Well, if it had been pushed down, the power take-off wouldn't have been running, would it?*

A. *No.*

Q. *So that was not what caused the tractor or the elevator to stop turning, was it?*

A. *No, the motor killed.*

Q. *So then we have to assume that the power take-off had not been disengaged at that point?*

A. *I couldn't say if it had been disengaged or not.*

Q. *Well, if it had been disengaged before the tractor stopped, the shaft wouldn't have been turning, would it?*

A. *No, that is right.*

Q. *And she wouldn't have gotten wound up in it, would she?*

A. *That is right.*

Q. *After you called Dr. Remsberg, did you talk to anyone else?*

A. *Yes, I called Arvid Anderson.*

Q. *Where does he live?*

A. *The first place north.*

Q. *About how far is that place from your place, as the crow flies?*

A. *Oh, about a mile.*

Q. *You hadn't touched anything at the place where this*

happened, had you?

A. No.

Q. *Did you call anybody else?*

A. *I called Kenny Walden, but I couldn't get him.*

Q. *Did you talk to anybody else?*

A. *Not right then.*

Q. *What did you do then?*

A. *I went back out to the tractor. I was rather hysterical over the deal.*

Q. *So what did you do?*

A. *Just stood there and waited.*

Q. *You just waited?*

A. *Yes. I felt Martha's hands and they were cold.*

Q. *Did she have her gloves on?*

A. No.

Q. *Had she been shoveling corn without gloves?*

A. *I don't remember that.*

Q. *Who was the first to arrive?*

A. *Arvid and Rueben Anderson.*

Q. *What was the first thing that you did?*

A. *I was standing there rather hysterical and Rueben walked over toward the elevator and he said, "I am sure she is dead, Clarence." And Arvid hung onto me, held onto my hand, my arm.*

Q. *Did the doctor arrive a little later?*

A. *Just shortly after, yes.*

Q. *Did Martha have any jewelry or watch on that day?*

A. *She had a watch, but I don't remember if she had it on that day.*

Q. *Do you have any other statement you would like to make?*

A. *No, I don't.*

Feikema then called Rueben Anderson to the stand.

Rueben testified that his father had called him to come downstairs; there was an accident at Larson's place and Clarence needed help. Rueben said he was downstairs by 5:15 a.m. His father probably got the call at about 5:10 a.m. They got in the car and drove toward Larson's residence, which is about five minutes away. Rueben estimated the time of arrival to be about 5:25. As they approached the driveway, they did not see the yard light on, but as they got closer, they saw the tractor lights on, lighting up the area around the elevator. Rueben said he jumped out of the car, saw the scene, and ran over to it. He assumed it was Martha there on the power shaft covered with a blanket. Rueben lifted it up and took a hold of her arm and it was cold; no sign of a pulse.

At this time Feikema made mention of the time and sequence of events up to this point for the jury to contemplate, but addressed the question to Rueben.

Q: *You were present, weren't you, when Mr. Larson said he got up about 4:40? And he went out and he started the tractor and got back in the house about 4:55, and that he then unthawed the elevator, which was about 5:20, approximately, and that he didn't start the elevator until about 5:25 or 5:30; but you say when you arrived there it was only five minutes after you had come downstairs and left the house?*
A: *About 5:10, then.*
Q: *All right, so at the most it would be 5:25?*
A: *Yes.*

Q. Can you see the Larson place from where you live?

A. Yes.

Q. Did you look out there when you got up?

A. Yes, we did.

Q. Were the lights on?

A. Not that I could see.

Q. Had you looked over there on other occasions when the yard light was on?

A. Yes, many times.

Q. Can you see clearly?

A. Yes.

Q. Did you see any lights on at all on the way over to the farm?

A. No, I didn't.

Q. Did you see any lights on when you got to the farm?

A. Yes.

Q. Where were they?

A. On the tractor.

Q. How much of an area did they light up?

A. They lit up quite a distance back, and the area around the elevator.

Q. When you arrived, what was the first thing that you did?

A. Well, I jumped out of the car and I see what it was so I ran over there.

Q. And what did you see?

A. She was there on the power shaft covered with a blanket.

Q. She was covered with a blanket?

A. Yes.

Q. Did you remove the blanket?

A. Not all the way. I lifted it up and took hold of her arm.

Q. Did you feel anything?
A. No. I felt and it was cold. I couldn't feel any pulse or anything.
Q. How long does it take to get from your place?
A. Not over five minutes.

Rueben said he noticed blood on the ground underneath the drawbar of the power shaft. He stated there was about six inches of snow on the ground around the tractor, and there were some slippery spots at the lower end of the elevator where it had been thawing out. Around the housing at the back of the tractor, there was just snow. Rueben said he left for a while and went down to the neighbors to get some more help. He woke him up and told him about the accident, then ran home to get some tools to get Martha loose. Rueben noticed Martha was wearing lightweight woolen gloves when he assisted in removing her from the power take-off. She had on a pair of slacks and a heavy coat.

Feikema called Dr. Robert Remsberg as his next witness. Dr. Remsberg testified that he was a licensed physician practicing in Tracy. He also lived in that area.

Q. You were called to the home of Clarence and Martha Larson on December 19, is that correct?
A. That is right.
Q. Do you recall the approximate time that you received this call?
A. Well, I had just gotten home from another call around 4:30, and I had gotten to bed and gotten to sleep and the phone rang. I wasn't sure whether it was the phone or doorbell, but it rang again and I didn't look

at the time immediately. It was, I know, 5:30 before I got out of the house, according to the cuckoo clock there and that makes a considerable commotion, and it struck 5:30 before I was dressed and left.

Q. So, then you would have received the call sometime before five?

A. A few minutes beforehand.

Q. All right. And you drove directly out to the farm. Is that correct?

A. Well, I went out there and I knew I was close to it, and I think I stopped at Andersons there, to find out, and I saw the car drive into his driveway there, and I stopped there and he told me where to go, and I went ahead and he followed me on back.

Q. I see, so that would have been the second time; second time that Rueben had left home that morning?

A. That is right. I saw him going into the drive.

Q. I see.

A. Which was close to the home.

Q. All right. Would you say that the description of how Martha Larson was first found was as you found her, as well as, when you drove up?

A. Well, approximately. As nearly as I could determine it.

Q. And would you describe the examination that you made of her at that time?

A. Well, the blood was still dripping slowly. Her hands were cold—I don't like to judge the temperature, but my estimation might be more accurate than a farmer's, who is out in the weather all the time; I know it felt like, with that wind that was blowing that morning, I would estimate it closer to five or ten above zero. And *that wind and snow was blowing pretty hard.*

Q. *And were her hands still cold?*

A. *Her hands. I didn't notice any gloves on them. There might have been. But when you got inside of her—*

Q. *Excuse me, sir. When you arrived, she was covered with a blanket?*

A. *She had a blanket and that heavy blue corduroy storm coat.*

Q. *All right. And—*

A. *When I got next to her chest, it was warm and you could hear her fibrillary twitching there with the stethoscope, and the blood was still dripping. It hadn't stopped bleeding completely.*

Q. *Did you check the site of the injury to the back of her head?*

A. *Not at the time that she was wound up in the—*

Q. *Afterward, did you?*

A. *I didn't check as far as checking to see whether it was caused from a broken neck or anything specific, but it seemed to be quite a bloody mass in there with hair and everything, and congealed and clotted blood covering it. I never cleaned it out.*

Q. *So could you determine from that examination whether or not the tissue was or had been torn in that area?*

A. *Well, it had to be torn, sir, or it wouldn't have bled like that.*

Q. *Well, what I am speaking of, sir, is the kind of injury to the back of the head. Was it a clean cut, or was it a mass of torn flesh, or was it—*

A. *I never cleaned the blood off and looked at the base of the—*

Q. So you couldn't tell us that, could you?

A. If that was the cause of her death? I couldn't swear to that.

Q. At that time you stated you heard, or with the stethoscope you heard some—what did you call it?

A. Fibrillary twitching.

Q. Fibrillary twitching of the arteries?

A. That is right.

Q. Would you say that she was still alive when you arrived?

A. Well, sir, that is a difficult question. When did she die?

Q. Was she still breathing?

A. I couldn't see that there was any respiratory movement. No.

Q. Were there any movements in her eyes?

A. No. Her eyes were open but there was no evidence of light reflex.

Q. Had she still been living, she would have had that reflex?

A. Not necessarily. In deep unconsciousness they generally don't have them.

Q. Would she have had breathing?

A. Well, sure. They would have breathing but you might not notice or be able to be aware of it.

Q. After you had concluded your examination, did you talk to Mr. Larson?

A. Yes. I went in the house there. He must have called the wife's sister before; they were there before I got there.

Q. Did you tell him at the time that his wife was dead?

A. I told him, and her sister and her husband, that there was no question but that she was dead.

Q. *Was there a question in your mind when you first arrived as to whether or not she was still then living or not?*

A. *That is right.*

Q. *There was still a question in your mind?*

A. *That there was a possibility, because, when you hit the chest with the heel of your hand, you could get that heart to beat a few times, but you couldn't get it to— you couldn't get at her, the way she was lying there with everything, and I thought if you got her out, you might be able to get her heart started, because you can sometimes with external massage start up the heart. It was twitching and fibrillating, but I couldn't sustain it any better, or any more than two or three beats of the heart, then it would go into a flutter.*

Q. *Did you ask them to remove her from the apparatus?*

A. *I certainly did.*

Q. *And this was to assist you in your examination?*

A. *No, not examination. Trying—if it was known that she had a chance to live, she wasn't going to live wound up in that stuff.*

Q. *Okay, and the ambulance or hearse arrived while you were there?*

A. *When Mr. Larson called me, I asked him if he wanted me to call an ambulance. He told me that there had been an awful accident out there. Well, I didn't ask him any questions or anything about what kind of an accident had happened. I asked him if he wanted me to call the ambulance and he said yes, he would. My wife called while I was dressing.*

Q. *So they arrived—*

A. *They got there soon after I did.*

Q. *What disposition was made of Martha Larson or her remains?*

A. *We asked Mr. Larson where he wanted her taken before—you couldn't do too satisfactory an examination out there, and by that time there were considerably more people showing up and he requested that they take her to Swenson's Mortuary at Balaton.*

Q. *Did you go directly and did the ambulance driver take her there then?*

A. *Yes. They were there when—*

Q. *When he said—*

A. *When I was talking to him.*

Feikema: Doctor, that will be all. The doctor was not sure how many miles it was to the Larson farm from his residence, but it took some time to get there.

Feikema called his next witness, Morris C. Ohman.

Q. *So in the month of December 1961, you went out to the home of Clarence Larson, did you not? Is that right?*

A. *Yes.*

Q. *And at that time, you were with someone else, were you?*

A. *Yes.*

Q. *And who—*

A. *Butson.*

Q. *And at that time you picked up the body of Martha Larson. Is that right?*

A. *Yes.*

Q. *You didn't have anything to do with extracting her*

from the power take-off shaft?

A. *No. The farmers that were there did that.*

Q. *And what happened? Did you deliver her then to the Swenson Mortuary at Balaton?*

A. *Yes.*

Q. *Did you either add anything or take anything from her personal effects at the time?*

A. *No, we helped him get her undressed and—*

Q. *Did you notice whether or not she was wearing a watch?*

A. *Yes. She had a gold watch.*

Q. *And what was done with the watch?*

A. *It was left there, I believe.*

Q. *Did you notice the time, as it was on the watch, at that time?*

A. *I did, but I don't know as I can accurately say now. It was either—I think it was ten minutes after four or something like that. I believe, but I wouldn't swear to it.*

Q. *Would ten minutes to four be more accurate?*

A. *I don't know which it was. One way or the other. I don't remember. I know there was a comment made about it, that the watch was stopped, but I don't remember just which way it was.*

Q. *And it wasn't running when you saw it?*

A. *I don't know.*

The next witness called was Vernon Butson.

Q. *What is your occupation?*

A. *Mortician.*

Q. *Which mortuary do you work, sir?*

A. Ohman Funeral Home.

Q. On the morning of December 19, 1961, you were out at the home of Clarence Larson?

A. That is right.

Q. And you helped pick up the remains of Martha Larson at that time?

A. That is right.

Q. And delivered it where?

A. Swenson's Funeral Home in Balaton.

Q. Was she still on the drawbar when you first saw her?

A. Yes.

Q. Was she wearing any gloves at that time?

A. We removed a glove at Swenson's Funeral Home. I helped remove the clothing there.

Q. And from which hand did you remove the glove?

A. From the left hand.

Q. Did you see any blood on her person?

A. A slight trickle from her mouth.

Q. Other than that, was there any blood on her face?

A. No.

Q. You noticed some at the back of her head a little later, though?

A. Yes.

Q. And you say that you assisted in removing her clothing, is that right?

A. That is right.

Q. Do you recall whether or not she had any jewelry removed from her body?

A. A wrist watch.

Q. And do you know which wrist the watch was on?

A. Well, I think it was on the left.

Q. Do you recall what time the watch read at the time

VICTIMS OF FOUL PLAY

you removed it?

A. I'd say around four o'clock.

Q. Was the watch running when you removed it?

A. No.

Q. How did you know that it was not then running?

A. Well, I couldn't answer.

Q. Did the hands stay in the same position?

A. They seemed to, yes.

Q. Do you recall whether or not it was slippery around the drawbar or tractor?

A. No.

Q. Any ice around there that you noticed?

A. I would say it was packed snow from what I observed.

Q. Okay, that is all.

JUROR NO. 2:

Q. Was the watch damaged?

A. It didn't seem to be. The crystal wasn't broken, I don't recall.

Q. (by Mr. Feikema) What was done with the watch?

A. Mr. Swenson kept all the personal affects.

Feikema called his last witness, Dr. John I. Coe. The doctor was pathologist and director of the laboratory at Minneapolis General Hospital, and a diplomate in forensic pathology, which is a separate branch. Pathology is the science employed both to assist the living, as well as, to determine the cause of death in those who have died. It refers to the studies of the causes and effects of disease, both as it effects the body and the microscopic aspects of the various fluids of the body. Dr. Coe's testimony dealt the most damaging blows to Larson's statements of how Martha died.

Q. *Did you perform an autopsy upon the remains of Martha Larson?*

A. *Yes, sir.*

Q. *Very briefly, can you describe your observations upon examination?*

A. *Well, there was evidence of a fracture in the upper portion of the right arm with a banded like area of leathery consistency on the skin of the arm, and over the front and side of the chest, on the right, which contrasted with the area of bruising over the right hip. Now, this latter looked like the ordinary bruise. That is, it had a purplish color, whereas these areas of compression that were found in the skin over the chest and arm did not show any evidence of bleeding into the skin, which is what causes the purplish color.*

Upon re-examining the internal contents—since the examination which I performed was an autopsy after a previous one had been done—there were noted to be multiple fractures of the ribs on the right side. They involved most of the ribs on the right, and were found in the lateral aspect. In other words, behind and more or less underneath the arm. Because of embalming techniques, these fractures were difficult to visualize, since large amounts of putty-like material had been used. But then when this was cleared away as well as it could be, there was very little evidence of bleeding about these fractures of the ribs.

The head was examined by opening the skull cap through the same incision that the previous pathologist had made, and there was evidence of bleeding beneath the skin of the scalp and beneath the fibrous coating that covers the scalp bone, known as the Galea. There were multiple fractures in the back of the skull with several pieces completely separated from the others, and more or less lying loosely. One of these consisted of a nearly circular fracture about three-quarters of an inch in diameter, in which there was evidence that this fragment of bone had been driven in, since the diameter of the bone on the outside was much smaller than the diameter of piece of bone on the inside. Only three-quarters of this hole, or this defect was present. The other fracture line didn't come in, so we couldn't find the small piece that fit in there. Upon examining the fractures or fracture, of the right arm, it was revealed that the muscle at the site of this fracture had been damaged by movement of the ends of the bone. Kind of chewed up, in a manner of speaking, but there was no bleeding at this site.

Microscopic sections were run of the muscle near the site of fracture and revealed no evidence of any injury to muscle that could be considered to have occurred prior to death. Sections were run of the brain which revealed evidence of some bleeding beneath the coating of the brain, but none in the brain substance itself. Sections of the skin over the chest where it had that leathery like area, revealed evidence of marked pressure effect, but no evidence of true bruising, and was in contrast to the microscopic appearance of the sections over the right hip.

Further examination of the organs was not attempted in this case because they had been previously examined and were rather markedly cut up from the previous examination.

Q. *Let's start with the bruise on the hip. This bruise was caused during the period of time that Mrs. Larson was alive yet, is that right?*

A. *Yes.*

Q. *And you could tell this for what reason?*

A. *Because there was rupture and bleeding into the tissues.*

Q. *If you damaged or put the same force of pressure upon the flesh of a dead person as you put upon the flesh of a live person—the one will bruise, will it not?*

A. *Yes, sir.*

Q. *And upon the dead one, it will not bruise?*

A. *Not bruise.*

Q. *There will be no evidence of any force having been put upon it, unless there is a break in the tissue. Is that right?*

A. *That is right.*

Q. *Had these pressure marks been caused during the period of time when she was living, would they also have bruised the tissue?*

A. *We would have expected it to, yes.*

Q. *But you didn't find any such bruises?*

A. *No, sir.*

Q. *You didn't find any evidence of bleeding in the area of these pressure marks?*

A. *No, sir.*

Q. *Nor did you find any evidence of bleeding from what you described as the pressure marks. Were there any on her body anywhere else?*

A. *No.*

Q. *Just on the arm. Is that correct?*

A. *No. There was no evidence of bleeding on the pressure marks on the body or on the arms. Either one.*

Q. *I see, and you would normally have expected to have found those?*

A. *Yes, sir.*

VICTIMS OF FOUL PLAY

Q. Let us assume that these injuries or these pressure marks were placed there simultaneously with the time that the injury to the back of the head; would you normally have expected to find bleeding?

A. You might not.

Q. You might not?

A. That is right.

Q. Let us go to the injury to the back of the head, the punched-out area that you have described.

A. Yes, sir.

Q. Was this injury of such a kind and nature to have caused her death?

A. I think it could have been. Certainly, the multiple skull fractures were evidence of damage to the brain and undoubtedly caused her demise.

Q. Then there were no other injuries to her body other than the injuries to the back of her head, which caused her death?

A. No, sir.

Q. Now you have described the injury to the broken arm?

A. Yes, sir.

Q. You said you examined it both visually and microscopically, the muscle; is that correct?

A. Yes, sir.

Q. In neither case did you find any evidence of bleeding, is that correct?

A. I did not.

Q. Would you normally have expected to have found bleeding in that area had that injury occurred simultaneously with the injury to the back of the head?

A. I would.

Q. Even had it occurred within a few moments of one or

the other; is that correct?

A. Yes.

Q. There would still be sufficient blood pressure within the veins and capillaries, so as to cause bleeding if they had been broken. Is that right?

A. There might be blood pressure, but you wouldn't even need blood pressure, because the blood does not clot inside the body for some period of time after death, and it is therefore possible that if you tear a vessel, bleeding will occur after death for some period of time, and also in any area in which we have a fractured bone, we will have torn such vessels, so even if you have fractures that occur at the time of death, we would usually find some bleeding around the site of the fracture.

Q. There is another area of the body where other fractures occurred, and you again found no evidence of bleeding. Is that correct?

A. At the fracture of the ribs, I found little evidence of it, although, as I said, my examination of this was not as good as I could have wished, because of the embalming procedures.

Q. Can you say that even if a person's arm has been fractured for some time after death, you would still get bleeding into the site of the fracture?

A. Well, not for too long a time after death.

Q. Well, that is what I am trying to learn. Is there any way of measuring that at all?

A. No. That will vary with individual people, depending on how their blood tends to clot, clotting and other circumstances, not all of which we know. One can only say that with a fracture occurring just before or *at the time of death, it is accompanied by bleeding. Fractures that occur a half hour after death, rarely show it at the site, but then one has to say that occasionally fractures that occur a considerable time after death, may show bleeding, in a few individuals, but on the other hand, I have seen no cases in which the fractures have occurred at the time of death, in which we have had bleeding. So, the reverse is not true. In other words, we may have bleeding at the site of the fracture that has occurred after death, for some period of time in a few individuals, but I have never seen the reverse. That is, an absence of bleeding from a fracture that occurred at the time of death.*

Q. *In other words, where you have a fracture which occurs simultaneously with the time of death, at the same time—*

A. *Yes.*

Q. *You know of no instance where you have ever seen a lack of bleeding at the site of fracture?*

A. *That is correct. It simply indicated to me that the fracture of the arm occurred after the person was dead.*

Q. *I see. You made some comments in your report. Could you state these comments and explain what each one of them means?*

A. *I wrote at the end of my report, the information from the examination which supported the following conclusions:*

1. *That at least some of the injuries to the skull and the bruise of the right hip, were sustained antemortem; in other words, before the patient died.*

2. *That one injury to the skull indicated the bone was struck by an essentially round object*

approximately 1.5 centimeters in diameter—this is about three quarters of an inch—which was a punched-out button of bone. Other fractures were consistent with blunt trauma, there wasn't anything that drove in a piece of bone, they were just fractures that would have resulted from striking a flat surface.

3. *That the fracture to the right arm, the skin changes on the chest, and probably the rib fractures, occurred post-mortem (after death).*

4. *That there was no fracture to the right pelvis, as had been reported in the first autopsy.*

Dr. Coe reiterated that in his opinion—death was caused by multiple fractures to the back of the head, any one of which would have been enough to cause death. Fractures of the ribs, bruises on the arm, and the broken arm, were all caused after death.

Before jurors went into deliberations, Dr. Patterson asked if any jurors had questions.

Juror No. 1 asked for clarification of when the blanket was placed over Martha. Rueben Anderson testified that when he arrived on the scene, the blanket was already on Mrs. Larson. But Mr. Larson testified that the blanket was not on Martha at the time the Andersons arrived.

Juror No. 1 asked, "Was the tractor running at the normal rate of speed for elevating at the time Mrs. Larson was supposedly caught?"

Mr. Larson replied, "Yes, at the normal speed to run the elevator."

Juror No. 3 asked, "Are we led to believe that she (Martha) was tangled up with her right arm alone in the drive or tumbling rod?"

Mr. Larson replied, "That is correct, right arm alone around the slip clutch where it slips in."

Juror No. 3 was confused about the times—the time Mr. Larson got up and the time the doctor was called. There was some confusion as to the exact time things happened, as no one watched the clock. It was estimated that 45 to 55 minutes had passed, during which all the events had taken place before Martha's death. It was estimated that the doctor was called just before 5:00 a.m.

Juror No. 4 asked, "What was the reason for doing this so early in the morning? It was pretty dark at that time of day. This was never brought up in the questioning."

Mr. Larson said, "The elevator belonged to Mr. Bennett. I don't know the boy's name, but the late Harold Bennett, and he came over the night before and he came over just after he had finished the chores, just before dark and we had tried to start the tractor the night before and I couldn't start it and that is why I tried the next morning. I figured I had flooded it or choked it too much. That is why I tried it the next morning, and my wife said, 'Leave it running and I will help you get that up. It isn't very much and you can get the elevator back in the morning.' I was disturbed that Harold Bennett had asked for the elevator back, and that is why I elevated it that morning."

The jury received their instructions from Dr. Patterson as follows:

"Upon inspection of the dead body and after hearing the testimony, and making needful inquiry, you shall draw up and deliver to the Coroner of this Inquisition, under your hand, in which you shall find and certify, when and how and by what means, the deceased person came to her death, and her name, if it is known, together with all the material circumstances attending her death, and if it appears that her death was caused by criminal violence; the jury shall further state who was guilty, either as Principal, or Accessory, if known, or who were in any manner the cause of her death, which inquisition, may be in substance as follows, and you will then follow the form which we have made out for you. Now, the determination of the jury may be either that it was accidental death, or death as a result of criminal violence, or you may make the determination that you are unable to determine the cause."

At 11:55 a.m., August 14, 1962, the jury retired for deliberation, and at 2:05 p.m. that day, the coroner's jury reconvened and the jury submitted its findings to the coroner as follows: "After due deliberation and from the evidence presented to the jury, we are unable to determine when or by what means Martha Larson met death. We do feel a skull fracture and brain injuries caused her death."

This matter was the first case of this nature that had been brought to the attention of a coroner's jury in Murray County and was one of the very few ever to have been handled in the history of the county.

LARSON INDICTED
AND ARRESTED

ON DECEMBER 4, 1962, a 23-member grand jury was presented with the evidence by County Attorney Jay Schueller, assisted by Special Assistant Attorney General Henry Feikema, and County Attorney Paul Fling of Slayton. The presiding judge was L.J. Irvine of Fairmont. After reviewing all the evidence, Clarence Larson, was indicted on a charge of first-degree murder. The grand jury action brought to a climax nearly a year of investigation by the state crime bureau and local law enforcement agencies. Murray County Sheriff, William Neumann, arrested Larson on the murder charge at a Tracy residence that evening. He appeared before Judge Irvine in Slayton that same evening, but the arraignment was postponed until Thursday, December 6, enabling the accused to secure legal counsel. Clarence Larson was placed in the Lyon County Jail after failure to post a $25,000 bond.

On December 6, Judge Irvine appointed O.T. Bundlie, Jr. of Pipestone as defense counsel. Bundlie filed a motion for a "change of venue" in January 1963, claiming the crime had received such widespread publicity throughout Murray and Nobles county newspapers that it would be unlikely that a fair and impartial jury could be selected. Bundlie told the Murray County Herald newspaper reporter that a hearing regarding the change of venue would be held before District Judge Charles A. Flinn in February, but Murray County Attorney Paul Fling filed objections to the motion as prosecuting attorney in the case, and stated, "I definitely feel the people of this county are quite capable of passing judgment on the basis of the evidence to be offered without prejudice."

On February 4, Judge Charles A. Flinn of Windom granted the change of venue and set Cottonwood County as the place where the trial would be held on March 4, 1963. In granting the change of venue, Judge Flinn cited what he considered to be improper reporting in both the Murray County Herald and the Worthington Daily Globe. The heavy area of circulation of the two newspapers proved to be a deciding factor. Because of the change of venue, witnesses and exhibits would travel from Murray County to Windom. Larson was being held in the county jail at Pipestone where his attorney's office was located, but was eventually transferred to the jail in Windom by Sheriff Neumann to await his trial. He remained in the custody of Sheriff James Ryan until the completion of the trial. Despite the change of venue, trial costs would still be the responsibility of Murray County.

THE TRIAL

On every murder case I write about, it's important to read through the trial transcript. It's exciting to read actual witness testimonies in order to get a feel for the people involved, and learn intimate details of the crime. It's as if I'm sitting there in the courtroom, watching the story unfold right before my eyes.

I first requested a copy of the transcript in November 2017. The court administrator in Murray County could not locate it and referred me to Cottonwood County because of the change of venue, but the transcript wasn't there either. I checked with the Minnesota History Center in the archives department but was told they never received it from Murray County. The last place I checked was with district court in Lyon County; again, was told it could not be located. In speaking with the court administrator in Lyon County, I was told that each county sets up their own guidelines for retention of trial transcripts.

I was advised that if a case had been acquitted, chances were the file had been destroyed at some point, since the case could never be tried again. This was disappointing. So, I had to search the newspapers for a summary of courtroom proceedings during the trial. Details of the trial were found in the Citizen and Windom Reporter, *March 1963, and are reported below.*

The stage had been set with the empaneling of an all-male jury of twelve, and the wheels of justice were set in motion, as the murder trial of Clarence Larson got under-way before Judge Charles Flinn in district court at Windom, Cottonwood County on March 4, 1963. This marked the first murder case to be heard in the history of Cottonwood County and one that was expected to be filled with drama and emotion.

Forty prospective jurors were called before the jury was finally selected on Tuesday afternoon, March 5. It took nearly two days to complete the task of jury selection. The members of the jury were: Ed Brand, Clarence Senst, Raymond Marsh, Leland Johnson, Milton B. Hoehne, Ewald L. Schuelke, Richard P. Lohrenz, Arthur M. Jenson, Lawrence Bressler, Eli Kopperud, Leslie R. Winters, and Emmett Witt. Gordon Klaseus was chosen as the alternate juror. Those chosen were farmers or men with farming backgrounds. It was evident that attorneys from both sides desired men who were familiar with farm machinery.

After jury selection, the judge reminded the jurors that the defendant is presumed innocent until proven guilty "beyond a reasonable doubt." He cautioned them not to discuss the case with anyone, but to judge the case solely on the

Clarence Larson at trial in Windom
(photo from Citizen and the Windom Reporter, March 6, 1963)

THE TRIAL

47

testimony presented after careful deliberation.

Janet Larson, defendant's daughter, and Richard Larson, a nephew, on leave from the US Navy, arrived March 5 to be with Larson during the trial. Larson appeared at the opening session of court, clean-shaven and dressed in a conservative blue suit. He showed no emotion as the indictment was read, but paid close attention as the prospective jurors were being questioned and frequently made notes on a pad he had in his possession.

Assisting defense attorney Bundlie, in the questioning of jurors, was P.R. Griebler, a Windom attorney. He was there because of his knowledge of citizens in the county. Representing the state was Paul Fling, Murray County attorney and Henry Feikema, Edina attorney and assistant attorney general.

Completion of the trial was expected within two weeks. Judge Flinn said that if the case didn't proceed rapidly enough, he would order longer daily sessions and Saturday sessions, if necessary.

Henry Feikema, in his opening statement to the jury, said the State would present testimony from two doctors who performed autopsies on the body, both of whom concurred that wounds, other than head injuries, were inflicted after death had occurred. But Larson contended that the death of his wife resulted when she became entangled in the power take-off of a tractor when the couple was elevating corn. Injuries to the victim included several head wounds, a broken arm, a compression wound on the hip, and several broken ribs. The State claimed that Larson killed his wife by striking her on the head with an unknown instrument.

The first witness to appear on the stand was Michael

Jost, former Murray County Engineer. He told of preparing a scale map of the Larson farmstead and a profile map of the terrain between the Larson home and the home of Arvid Anderson, a neighbor. Jost said the profile map showed a direct line of sight from a window in the Anderson home to an electric yard light in Larson's yard. His testimony also noted that some trees extending higher than the line of sight stood between the two homes.

The second witness called to the stand was John Kuhlman, telephone company manager at Slayton. He said Larson's phone had been disconnected on December 9, 1961 because the phone bill remained unpaid. He stated that three calls had been made from the farm on December 19, all three to Dr. Robert Remsberg of Tracy, at 5:14 a.m., 4:13 p.m. and 5:45 p.m. the day Mrs. Larson was killed. Kuhlman said the phone could have been put back into operation by replacing two fuses which had been removed or by connecting the fuse terminals with any conducting material. It was suspected that Clarence stole two fuses from a neighbor's phone box some time before December 19 so he could make telephone calls early that morning.

The first witness called March 6, was Arvid Anderson. He gave the lengthiest testimony of the witnesses and gave a complete recollection of the events from 5 a.m. the day of the alleged murder when he was awakened by a telephone call from Mr. Larson. "We have had an accident over here. Come over as fast as possible," Anderson quoted the urgent phone call. Anderson, accompanied by his son, Rueben, said they arrived in a few minutes and saw Martha's body wrapped around the power take-off. He testified the body was covered by a blanket. He said there was some blood and hair on the drawbar, but did not recall seeing any blood on the snow. "Clarence told me, 'I have called the doctor and Albert and Bertha (Nelson).'" Anderson said he also used the Larson phone to call another neighbor. Rueben left to summon more help while Anderson and Larson walked to the house. Then Larson started to cry and said he thought he was going to faint. Anderson stated that he had purchased the Larson farm in the early part of December 1961 and the transaction was completed on January 8, 1962 for $150 per acre. He had been negotiating with Larson since the previous summer.

That afternoon, Dr. Remsberg took the stand. He said he received a call from Larson about 5:15 a.m. on the morning of Martha's death and hurried to the farm after telling his wife to call an ambulance. He said that Mrs. Larson was technically alive when he examined her. When he checked the chest with the stethoscope, he thought he heard a heartbeat. He said he could feel a twitching of the muscles in her chest when he struck the heart area. He further stated that he found no sign of breathing and no reflex from the eyes. After the body was placed in the ambulance, he said there was no sign of life. The doctor was cross-examined by O.T. Bundlie. Remsberg stated that muscle twitching is common for some time after death and that erratic heartbeats would be possible as long as fifteen minutes after death.

Witness Dale Bennett, another neighbor of Larsons, owned the elevator and told the jury that he had stopped at the Larson farm the previous day and said he would like to have the machine returned. Larson told him he would finish the job the next morning and see that it was brought to the owner's farm.

VICTIMS OF FOUL PLAY

Morris Ohman of Tracy testified that he helped remove the body and take it by ambulance to the Swenson Funeral Home in Balaton with the assistance of Vernon Butson. He said he helped the mortician remove the clothing and watch from the body and noted that the watch read either ten minutes to four or ten minutes after. He also told of the bleeding from the head wound while the body was lying on the stretcher.

Earl Swenson, Balaton mortician, was the final witness for the State that day. He identified the woman's clothing and said he began the embalming process after the ambulance men had departed. He also commented on the watch, saying that it had stopped at 3:50 and showed no signs of damage. Swenson said that he moved the body to Sioux Valley Hospital, Sioux Falls, the following day on orders of Dr. Hugh Patterson, Coroner, where an autopsy was to be performed by Dr. John Alexander. He said he later returned the body to Murray County for the coroner's inquest and subsequent funeral. Swenson also stated that the wound on the back of the head showed signs of bleeding when it arrived at the mortuary.

Several of these witnesses testified that they had known the Larsons for many years and knew of no difficulties between them. They also said they saw no signs of a struggle at the Larson farm.

Vernon Butson was the first to testify the following morning. He stated he accompanied Morris Ohman to the Larson farm to help remove the body.

Sheriff Neumann testified that he was not personally acquainted with Larson before the death of his wife, but he had called at the farm several times in the preceding two months to serve some legal papers but failed to find Larson home. Neumann learned of the death that morning and went to the farm that afternoon and talked with Larson's nephew, Richard. Later, after conferring with Coroner Patterson, Sheriff Neumann called the Crime Bureau. That evening he returned to the farm and discussed the accident with Larson. Neumann called at the farm several times following December 19, and said Larson was cooperative in the questioning.

Next to testify was Coroner Dr. Hugh Patterson, with the main subject of discussion being the wrist watch worn by Martha. Patterson said the watch was given to him by mortician Earl Swenson at about 10:15 p.m. on December 19, and that the watch was stopped with the hands pointing to 3:51. Patterson stated that the next morning he took the watch to a Slayton jeweler and that it had started running, although it had not been wound by him or anyone else.

Jeweler Erickson was then called and stated that the watch was undamaged and continued to run, but it was not uncommon for an inexpensive watch of Mrs. Larson's type to stop when struck by a sudden jar and to later start again when jarred a second time.

Testimony was given by Crime Bureau Agent John Barry. It was revealed that Larson had told him he had decided to take his wife to work the next morning and that he had hooked up the disconnected telephone so that Martha could call the person with whom she usually rode, to tell them of the change in plans. The rest of Barry's testimony was a reiteration of what Larson claimed happened on the day of Martha's death.

Testimony by one of the state's key witnesses, Dr. John

W. Alexander, pathologist, revealed that in his opinion, Mrs. Larson died of head injuries, and that the other injuries on her body were sustained after death. As the result of the autopsy performed by him on Mrs. Larson's body December 20, 1961 at Sioux Falls, he said that a person suffering an injury such as the skull fracture would have died within minutes or an even shorter time, and also said that lack of bleeding by bone fragments from the ribs penetrating into the chest cavity would be related, in his opinion, to a post-mortem injury. In further testimony, Dr. Alexander stated that there was no brain damage to the front of Mrs. Larson's brain. From this evidence, he said, in his opinion, the injury was sustained by a moving object striking a stationary skull, rather than a moving skull striking a stationary object. He said that, had the latter been the case, there would have been damage to the front of the brain.

Next to take the stand was Dr. John Coe, pathologist at Minneapolis General Hospital, who prefaced his testimony by relating that he does most of the autopsy work in Hennepin County and does about 700 of them a year. Coe then related that his examination of the body bore out the same general findings related by Dr. Alexander, following his examination of Mrs. Larson's body in April 1962, and agreed that the cause of death was a skull fracture and that death would have been very rapid, "less than five minutes." Under cross-examination, Coe was asked whether the injury to the head could have been caused by the head of a bolt, a rounded corner on the tractor or some other portion of the power take-off. He said any of them could have caused such an injury, but "only if the skull was stationary and the object was in motion." Bundlie cross-examined Dr. Coe concerning the difficulties of performing an autopsy on a body after it had been interred for a period of time, and after a previous autopsy had been performed. In his cross-examination of Dr. Alexander, Bundlie inquired about the fact that because the right arm was twisted over and around the take-off shaft, it might have resulted in a "tourniquet action" to restrict bleeding from the arm injuries. Dr. Coe refused to agree that this would affect the examination he conducted on the arm.

On March 11, special prosecutor Henry Feikema called his final witnesses to the stand. Among them was Duane Wetter of Tracy, service manager for an International Harvester dealer. When asked, in his opinion, if an International tractor such as Larson's, generating 40 hp using the power take-off, could be stopped by a 150 lb. body caught in the PTO, he replied that it would not. He testified that his opinion was based on at least three incidents of this type of which he knew.

Two members of the carpool in which Martha Larson rode to work were called to the stand, with one stating that she had never known Mr. Larson driving his wife to work previously, and that Martha Larson had never told them of any difficulties she might be having at home, but that she was not the type of person who would discuss such matters.

Clarence Larson was called to the stand on March 12 at 10:35 a.m. by attorney Bundlie. At times, he was visibly moved during the questioning and had to pause to wipe his eyes with a handkerchief before continuing. While on the stand, he told of the incidents before and after the death of his wife on December 19, 1961. His testimony was the same as what was reported at the coroner's inquest; except for a few new discoveries revealed in Larson's testimony as follows:

The defendant was asked about insurance policies, and stated that both he and his wife had life insurance.

Asked about the condition of the ground, Larson said there was about six inches of snow in the yard and the area around the elevator was sloppy and slippery, caused by the water that had run out of the elevator. To the best of his knowledge, the yard light was on all the time, although he said he didn't take any note of this. Larson said there was a two-way switch in the yard and house. He indicated that on previous occasions the light had been turned off from the house and that he had walked over to the garage to switch the light back on. He said it was possible that his wife could have turned it off when she turned the room light off, since both switches were located together.

After he made the phone calls, Larson said he rushed back to the elevator to check on Martha. Again, he said he checked her left arm and throat for signs of a pulse but couldn't find any. He said he also made another call to Mrs. Alfred Larson, his wife's sister, before Anderson arrived.

Asked whether he had turned off the power take-off lever, he said he could have pushed it down, but all he could think of was Martha lying there. When Dr. Remsberg arrived, he said the doctor gave him a sedative, which helped quiet down his nerves a bit.

Larson also talked about wanting to bring the body to the mortician at Balaton because it would be a shorter distance to the church and easier for the relatives to attend. He said it didn't come to his mind to call the sheriff and coroner at that time, but rather, he left everything to Dr. Remsberg. Some relatives arrived at the farm later that morning.

Asked about taking the elevator back to the owner and

the tractor to the garage, he said he had suggested that this be done when he was in the basement talking with friends. He said he and his children, Janet and Ronald, went to Balaton that afternoon, picked out a casket, and made funeral arrangements.

After returning home, he said a man from the telephone company came out to see that the phone was properly connected, and he believed that he had paid the man for the service at that time.

Later, Dr. Hugh Patterson, came out and asked for permission to perform an autopsy. He said he signed the document and another at the time of the second inquest. He said he had been ordered on many occasions to report to the courthouse for questioning during the following year and never refused; he always cooperated.

Larson testified that his marriage had been a happy one. He and his wife had married when they were eighteen and had raised two children during their thirty-two years together. Larson also told of being in an automobile accident on January 16, 1959 in which he suffered injuries which led to his decision to retire from farming, sell the farm, and move to town.

He stated that he and his wife had been sorting personal belongings the day before, in preparation for their move to Marshall. Later that day, his neighbor, Dale Bennett, had stopped by and asked to have his elevator returned. He promised to have it back the next day, he said. He informed Bennett that he tried to start the tractor to complete the job late that afternoon but it failed to start, so he had to postpone the job until the next morning.

Larson stated that he agreed to take his wife to Marshall

the next morning instead of riding with the carpool, since they had planned to take two sacks of vegetables to the home of their son in Marshall, and she didn't want to bother the women with this matter. He said he connected up the telephone so that his wife could tell the carpool driver that she would not be riding with her.

Prosecuting attorney, Henry Feikema, cross-examined Larson. Under questioning by Feikema, Larson again described his activities on the morning of his wife's death. Larson said he was on top of the corn crib when the elevator stopped. He crawled off the crib and walked around the tractor where he found his wife tangled around the power take-off of the machine.

"Did you try to remove her?" asked Feikema.

"She was wound tight in it," answered Larson. "I took ahold of the shaft. Everything was solid." Feikema asked Larson if it was not a fact that his wife died shortly before 4 a.m. "No," declared Larson.

He was asked about the auto accident in 1959 in which he was injured, and questioned about his wife's employment, pointing out that Mrs. Larson went to work for the Swift plant in Marshall in November 1958, four months before the auto accident, intimating that the need for her to seek employment occurred before his accident.

Under questioning by Feikema, Larson agreed that his wife had been staying at the home of her mother in Garvin three to four nights a week and sometimes at the home of her son in Marshall on Fridays and Saturdays. They had not attended church near Balaton for quite some time.

Relative to the auto accident in which Larson stated he was injured, the State's attorney called attention to the moving of a freezer from his home after his wife's death, to Ronald's home in Marshall. At that time, it required five men. Yet it was asserted that it required only two men to move the freezer to Mrs. Sande's home in Tracy later, when Larson assisted in the job. Larson maintained that he did not lift it alone, nor did he lift very much.

Questioned about the sleeping arrangement which had been in effect since Janet was eight or nine years old, he said he had continued to sleep downstairs while his wife slept upstairs. He said Janet had graduated from high school in 1961 and had rented a room in Tracy, returning to her home on weekends and on other occasions.

Feikema questioned him about connecting the telephone, the tractor, and the urgency involved with the elevator. Larson was questioned intensively about the time element surrounding the morning of December 19, and sought to prove that more time would be required to carry out all the tasks that were performed, had he not risen earlier.

Feikema also questioned Larson about the clothing Mrs. Larson wore and later delved extensively on the yard light question and circumstances surrounding the death of Mrs. Larson, in light of testimony given earlier by Larson.

Larson was questioned about his relationship with Mrs. Sande. Larson said he had been staying at her home from one to two nights a week. He said he had known her for about fifteen years and had visited her when she lived at Hibbing when he went on deer hunting and fishing trips. After Mrs. Larson's death, he and his daughter moved to her home, where he remained until his arrest.

In re-direct examination, the defense raised many questions, including the sleeping arrangement. He maintained that he was used to sleeping in his own bed, and Janet, who often came home unexpectedly on the weekends, always slept with her mother.

Larson stated that his wife's headaches came on suddenly, describing them as shooting pains in back of the head, "like an electric shock and she'd black out."

During cross-examination, Feikema questioned Larson about Mrs. Sande, in whose home he now resided in Tracy. Clarence stated that before her divorce, Jean had marital problems. "He threatened both Mrs. Sande and her daughter's life. He was a drunken maniac," said Larson. Mrs. Sande divorced her husband in 1952. Larson said he did not know of Jean's whereabouts until she moved to Pipestone in 1956. Larson said he had known Jean about fifteen years, as did his wife and daughter. He admitted that he had occasionally stayed overnight at the Sande residence and moved in with Jean in January 1962, less than a month after his wife's death. His daughter also stayed overnight on occasion and he said that there was no secrecy about the relationship, no clandestine affairs, nor hidden motives.

Larson said he had borrowed money from Mrs. Sande and repaid it without interest, and that he had helped contribute financially after he and his daughter moved to the large four-bedroom home in Tracy. He further stated that there was nothing of a romantic nature between him and Mrs. Sande before or after Mrs. Larson's death. Both he and his daughter had separate bedrooms in the home. Larson said he just couldn't stay at the farm after his wife's death and moved in with his wife's sister, Mrs. Alfred Nelson, but said the reason he moved a few days later, was because he overheard Mrs. Nelson saying that "we don't have to fuss very much when there are just the two of us here." He felt he had to find some other place to stay. He had other relatives, but they had families and it would be hard for them to find room. His daughter, who later attended beauty school in Sioux Falls and worked there, returned on occasion and stayed at the Sande home.

Feikema also questioned Larson about his relationship with Mrs. Sande, discussing her residence at Pipestone. Feikema asked Larson if Mrs. Sande had lived in a motel when she first arrived at Pipestone. "No, she did not," he answered. Larson also stated that he and his wife had separate bank accounts at a Marshall bank.

The obvious attempt by Feikema to establish a motive in the form of Mrs. Sande's relationship with Clarence Larson did not impress the court. Before his ruling, Judge Flinn said it was "not clear to me that we can say any motive can be proved."

During Larson's testimony, Mrs. Sande and her seventeen-year-old daughter, Olivia, sat in the front of the spectator area in the courtroom, which was packed.

As the defense wound up its presentation of the case, O.T. Bundlie told the court that he had one more question for Larson before resting the case. At that point he asked Larson to turn to the jury and tell them whether he had killed his wife. Larson slowly turned his head, looked at the jurors and said, "I did not kill my wife, so help me God. I did not," he declared. Larson's testimony ended at 3:27 p.m.

The defense finally rested its case after a week of testimony. Every day the courtroom was crowded with spectators, coming in as early as 8:00 a.m., with some bringing their lunch, so they would not lose a place in the spectators' section of the courtroom. Judge Flinn had special bailiffs on duty to maintain order. The judge also barred newspaper photographers from the courtroom proceedings.

After a short recess on March 12, a motion for a directed verdict of "not guilty" was made by defense counsel Bundlie, claiming the State had failed to produce sufficient evidence for prosecution, and that circumstantial and insufficient evidence would not support a conviction on a charge of first-degree murder, and on the grounds there was "reasonable doubt."

Henry Feikema and county attorney, Paul Fling, argued that the case should be considered by the jury. "There was a question for the jury to consider," he declared. "We oppose the motion." It was then presented to Judge Flinn, who moved that it be granted.

The case was abruptly brought to a conclusion sometime after 4 p.m. when the judge said that "the evidence was not sufficient to find the defendant guilty." Judge Flinn said he would have been obligated to set the jury's verdict aside in the event they had found Larson guilty.

Normally, the judge overseeing the case can alert the jury that they should vote for an acquittal instead of finding the defendant guilty or innocent. The jury must follow the judge's instructions and return with the verdict. In this case, the jury of twelve men did not have an opportunity to render their decision as the case culminated that afternoon.

After the judge announced his ruling, Janet Larson jumped from the front row of the spectator section of the courtroom and ran up and kissed her father. "Words cannot show how happy I am," she said.

Larson appeared to be in shock over the verdict. He said

his plans for the future had yet to be determined. He had spent almost 100 days in jail. In regard to the case, he said, "I want to give my attorney Bundlie all the credit in the world." This was Bundlie's first criminal case.

The judge's action brought a permanent close to the long, drawn-out affair, as there can be no appeal on the part of the State in any criminal action of this type. People in the surrounding areas felt a great injustice had been served in this case.

Murray County attorney Paul Fling reported to the newspaper "that the lengthy investigation of Larson was a sufficient reason for more and better law enforcement facilities and manpower on both the state and county level. Adequate facilities could have brought this matter to a close much sooner."

Clarence walked out of the courtroom with his daughter, into a crowd of spectators who were anxious to get a glimpse of the man who was acquitted of first-degree murder charges. Many in the crowd were screaming obscenities at Clarence and hollered out: "murderer, lock him up." The spectators felt Clarence got away with the cold-blooded, premeditated murder of his wife.

Thus, the first murder trial ever to be tried in Cottonwood County was concluded through the due process of the courts and Clarence Larson, charged with the murder of his wife, walked out of the courtroom a free man.

THOUGHTS ABOUT
THE INVESTIGATION

IN REVIEWING ALL the details regarding this case, it appears that proper procedures and protocols were not followed throughout this investigation, and many questions remain unanswered to this day.

I did a search online and found several websites that discussed the procedures to follow when an accidental death occurs at home. "If the death was unexpected or you aren't sure if the person was dead, call 911 immediately. Ask for an ambulance and explain the problem and describe the circumstances. Once the ambulance crew arrives, they will either contact the person's physician or the police. The physician will be needed to pronounce cause and time of death. When should the coroner be called? The coroner is required to investigate an accidental death, which appears suspicious or when unusual circumstances are involved. The coroner should be at the scene of the accident before the body is removed for an autopsy."

You would think Clarence should have called 911 first, but that emergency system wasn't developed until February 1968, so that explains why Clarence called Dr. Remsberg first, and then the neighbor, Arvid Anderson. Clarence stated that it didn't come to his mind to call the sheriff and coroner at that time, but rather left everything to Dr. Remsberg. Why didn't Dr. Remsberg call the coroner right away when he arrived at the scene? The doctor should have followed protocol when there was a death due to a suspicious accident. Another flaw in the process happened when the ambulance crew arrived. They helped remove the body from the machine and immediately delivered it to the Swenson Funeral Home in Balaton. The mortician started the embalming process before the coroner arrived. This again was another violation of protocol. The mortician should have known that the coroner had to do an autopsy on the body first before the embalming process could take place. Dr. Patterson didn't get permission to perform the autopsy until later that day, when he finally contacted Clarence at his residence. Clarence had to sign a document before the autopsy could be performed. And why did Clarence call Dr. Remsberg later that day at 4:13 p.m. and 5:45 p.m.? What would be the purpose of those calls? One can only imagine.

Gross mistakes were made during the investigation. First, the crime scene had been destroyed with people trampling through the area and bloody snow being covered up. It was unclear why Dr. Remsberg did not immediately call the sheriff when he arrived at the scene. He must have known it was imperative to have photographs taken of a possible crime scene.

Sheriff Neumann didn't even discuss the accident with Clarence until later that evening, after first conferring with Coroner Patterson and the Crime Bureau. It wasn't until December 28 when officers, along with Clarence, re-positioned the tractor on the property, as it was on December 19, and then took photographs, but apparently the elevator equipment, belonging to the neighbor, was not included, so the staging was incomplete. This partial re-enactment of the scene took place nine days after the accident.

It appears the investigation was flawed from the very beginning and details were not completed in a timely manner. Since the investigative files could not be located and were probably destroyed, we wonder if the sheriff ever did a thorough search of the Larson home, the basement, the outbuildings, or any of the tools or equipment used during the elevation of the corn that day; did the sheriff look for any blood evidence on the property; was the elevator or the power take-off mechanism checked to see if everything was working properly? Why weren't photographs taken of any of these areas on the day of the accident? Were the neighbors ever questioned, or were Janet or Ron ever interviewed to see if there was possibly domestic abuse going on in the family? I found out from family sources that Martha was afraid of Clarence. He may have had a bad temper. It was said that Martha's parents, and other family members, were afraid for her safety and pleaded with her on numerous occasions to move out and file for divorce, but for whatever reason, Martha did not heed their advice.

When Janet arrived home that day, it was rumored she saw signs of a struggle in the home. I do not know if this entailed seeing items tossed about in disarray, or if she discovered blood spatter inside the home, or outside in the yard, near the scene of the tragedy.

Another rumor suggests that either on the day of the viewing or at the funeral, Janet was hysterical. She was standing near her mother's casket, just sobbing uncontrollably. At one point, she turned and looked at her father and shouted, "You killed my mother." Allegedly, there were several people nearby who heard Janet's accusation.

It was also rumored that when Bertha Nelson arrived at the scene, she immediately suspected Clarence had something to do with her sister's death. I'm not quite sure whether Bertha mentioned her concerns to police investigators or anyone else at the time.

Another story I heard was that on the day after Martha's death, Clarence, Jean, and Olivia were seen at the Blue Mound Inn in Luverne having dinner. Someone seated nearby, in the restaurant, may have overheard the conversation, but at some point, during the evening, Clarence made the comment to Jean that, "everything had gone well," probably referring to the events that transpired the previous day regarding Martha's death.

Anyone can clearly see the timeline of events was suspect. All that transpired from 4:40 a.m. until Martha's death, clearly showed that Clarence had to have been up much earlier. And why was Martha's watch stopped at 3:50 a.m.? Could this have been the actual time of her death? The question remains—was Martha murdered by her husband, or did part of her clothing get caught up in the power take-off, causing the accident? I guess we will never know for sure what happened that cold December morning when poor Martha was found wrapped up in farm equipment.

THE POSSIBLE MOTIVE

FROM ALL THE testimony at the coroner's inquest and the murder trial, it was quite evident that Martha was most likely deceased before she was placed on the power take-off. We have to ask ourselves, what was the motive? The most logical motive would be for money.

During the trial, the attorney questioned Clarence regarding any life insurance on Martha. Clarence testified that he did have an insurance policy on Martha. There was the rumor that Martha had been heavily insured and that Clarence collected a substantial amount of money upon her death.

I had to do some investigating to see if I could find out just how much money Clarence received from the insurance company. I contacted the Lyon County courthouse and discovered that Clarence had filed a wrongful death suit on two insurance companies for their failure in paying accidental death benefits.

Well, it was not enough for me just to know that a suit had been filed; I wanted to get my hands on the actual file and read through those documents. I made an appointment with the court administrator at the Lyon County Courthouse in Marshall to review the case file.

It was a very cold day in February 2020, the day of my appointment. It was probably not the best day for me to be out and about, because the heater in my car wasn't working very well, so I was not only freezing half to death, but I had a hard time seeing out the fogged-up window too. Needless to say, it was a long, treacherous drive for me and when I made it home alive, the first thing I did was make an appointment with my mechanic to check out the car and replace the thermostat, which I suspected it needed.

But I finally made it to the courthouse on time, thank goodness, but my fingers and toes were numb. I could barely walk from the parking lot to the front door of the courthouse, I was in so much pain from the cold. I took the elevator to the third floor, where the file was at the counter waiting for me to review. Now that I had the file in my hands, I was anxious to take it to a quiet spot, sit in a comfy chair, and take my time reading through it, but that was not to be. The lady behind the glass partition said I had to stand at the counter and review it. I couldn't believe it! I had to stand on my painful feet the entire time, when there was a comfy chair just a few feet behind me. I asked if I could sit down there and the lady said, "No, you have to stand at the counter." I was mortified.

So, I stood there, slowly opened the file and began reading through the documents. I discovered that on January 26, 1959, Martha Larson applied for an accident insurance policy, naming Clarence as the beneficiary. The policy was written up by Duane Peterson, an insurance agent in Garvin. The National Fidelity Life Insurance Company was the insurer, and the policy became effective on January 28, 1959. "That among other provisions, said insurance policy insured Martha Larson against loss of her life by accidental bodily injury in the principal sum of $10,000."

Then on December 8, 1961, Clarence applied for a 31-day accident policy on Martha, naming him as the beneficiary. "That among other provisions, said policy insured Martha Larson against loss of her life by accidental bodily injury in the sum of $10,000." This became effective on December 8, 1961 at 9:30 a.m. Just think, less than two weeks before Martha's death, Clarence had applied for an accident policy. This type of policy must be renewed every 31-days.

Upon Martha's death, Clarence provided proof of loss to the insurance companies but as fate would have it, the companies neglected and refused to make any payment whatsoever. Failure to pay benefits might have been because of the suspicious nature of her demise, or there may have been a waiting period stipulated in the policy. I was not able to confirm this from the documents.

Clarence was acquitted in March 1963 and had to find a way to get his hands on all that money from the insurance companies. In May, he contacted his attorney, O.J. Bundlie informing him the insurance companies had refused to pay the claims. Bundlie drew up the documents for the complaint, which was filed in Lyon County, 5th Judicial Court on May 10, 1963. As written: "Clarence L. Larson vs. St. Paul Fire and Marine Insurance Company. Plaintiff (Larson) demands judgement against defendant (insurance company) for $10,000 plus interest from December 19, 1961, plus costs and disbursements in each instance. Action was served on defendant on May 13, 1963." A similar complaint was filed against National Fidelity Life Insurance Company with the same demands as stated above.

In December 1963, the suit was to be placed on the calendar at the next general term of district court for trial by jury. On January 14, 1964, a note in the file stated "that action was compromised and settled, and without further costs to any parties," so that means the suit was probably settled out of court for an undisclosed amount.

The story goes that Clarence was quite happy about winning the suit because he made a trip to the Garvin Bar with Jean that night. As soon as the couple was seated at the bar, Clarence told the bartender to give everyone a round of drinks to help him celebrate his big win. A reliable source told me that her parents were in the bar that night, and when they received their drinks, they immediately brought them up to the bar, slammed them down and said, "Keep your drinks paid with blood money." The couple walked out, along with other patrons in the bar that night.

INTERVIEWS WITH A
JUROR AND A WITNESS

As PART OF my investigation, I hoped to interview any jurors who might still be around that remembered details of the trial. Most members of the twelve-man jury were now deceased. It's been fifty-seven years since the days of the criminal trial, so I had doubts about finding anyone to interview, but my friend, Debra, located an address for Raymond Marsh, one of the jurors who was still alive, so I sent him a letter in February 2020 requesting an interview. I waited several weeks for a response. The letter was not returned to me as "undeliverable" so I figured Mr. Marsh received it and maybe did not want to talk about it or didn't remember details of the trial.

On April 16, 2020, I received a call from Mr. Marsh. I must tell you I was ecstatic to hear from him. Ray explained to me that the letter I sent him had ended up in someone else's mailbox and finally was delivered into his hands nearly two months later. At the time of the trial, Ray was thirty-one years old. He had a great sense of humor and his mind was as sharp as a tack. We had a nice conversation and he took me back to the days of the trial. Ray said this was the first and only time he had been a juror, and it happened to be on a criminal case. He remembered the courtroom being packed each day. He said that he and another juror, Clarence Senst, from Jeffers, carpooled to the courthouse every day during the week-long trial. Ray remembered the following key points from those days.

After closing arguments were presented, Ray said Judge Flinn called a short recess. When the judge returned to the courtroom later, he solemnly walked to the bench and slowly seated himself in the large, black leather chair. He bowed his head for a few moments, then turned to stare at the jurors, who were quietly seated in their chairs. Flinn said he had taken time in his chambers to review the case and then said, "The evidence was not sufficient to find the defendant guilty, so I am dismissing this case." Then the judge told the jurors he would like to speak with them in his chambers. This was highly unusual, and Ray said he wasn't quite sure why the judge wanted to talk with them, but they all quietly assembled into his huge office and were comfortably seated in front of him.

The judge was very cordial. He wanted to know their thoughts about the case. He asked them, "How would you have voted, guilty or not guilty?"

Ray said there was quite a bit of discussion amongst them at the time, but most of the jurors said they had too many doubts about the details of the case. The majority of the men said they would have probably voted "not guilty," but a few of them wanted to convict. Inevitably, this would have resulted in a "hung jury." Ray said that he was one that would not vote to convict because he felt the State had not presented enough evidence to make their case. He also stated the investigation was flawed from the very beginning, and this was what led to reasonable doubt in the minds of most of the jurors. Ray felt Judge Flinn was fair in his decision to dismiss the charges.

The witness I interviewed was Rueben Anderson. My friend Muriel introduced me to him and his wife, Jeane in June 2016. Rueben and his father were the first men on the scene the day of the tragedy. Rueben testified at the coroner's inquest and at Larson's criminal trial. He was thirty-one years old at the time of Martha's death. He has a vivid memory of the events of December 19, 1961. I have interviewed him on several occasions, discovering some amazing things.

On the day of the tragedy, Rueben remembered Clarence exiting the house as they drove up the long driveway. He saw the tractor and the elevator with what appeared to be Martha on the power take-off, covered with a blanket. Rueben jumped out of the car, ran over and felt Martha's wrist; she was very cold. Then he watched as Clarence and his father walked into the house. Rueben told me that as soon as his father entered the kitchen area, Arvid noticed some large blotches of what appeared to be blood on the floor. There just happened to be a scatter rug nearby. Clarence immediately placed his foot on the rug and dragged it over the bloody mess, hoping Arvid hadn't seen it.

Rueben said he was horrified by the bloody scene, as was his father. He took me back to that awful day and described the scene for me. He said "Martha was lying horizontal along the length of the metal shaft. Her body was covered with a blanket. Her head was near the rear end of the tractor. There was a large spike embedded in her clothing." Rueben said he felt the body was in a strange position on the PTO. Normally, if a person's clothing gets caught in the mechanism, they generally get wrapped around the shaft end-over-end, not lying lengthwise on the metal apparatus. Rueben said he felt this so-called accident had been staged. He noticed a large, bloody gash on the back of Martha's head; he was not sure what caused it. I asked him what tools were used to remove the body from the PTO. He told me that they did not have to use any tools to remove her body. Instead, when the ambulance crew arrived, Rueben, the crew, and Dr. Remsberg slowly and carefully unraveled her body, by hand, from the mechanism. No tools were needed at the time. Arvid also suspected Martha's death was no accident.

At some point that morning, Clarence asked Arvid if his son, Russell, could come over and help him clean up the bloody mess in the yard. Russell arrived at Clarence's home after he finished with his own morning chores. He brought the snow scoop along. Clarence directed him on where to place piles of fresh, clean snow over the bloody areas at the scene of the accident. Rueben remembered Clarence asking him if he would drive to Sioux Falls to pick up Janet at the Stewart Beauty School and bring her home.

Clarence instructed Rueben, "Don't tell Janet her mother's dead, just tell her she's sick."

Rueben said he went home to freshen up a bit, then traveled to Sioux Falls where he picked up Janet. She was quite surprised by the unexpected visit. As instructed, Rueben informed her that her mother was ill and she was needed at home. Janet thought it odd that her father had not made the trip, but she went along with the plan, knowing she'd find out all the particulars when she arrived home. Rueben said it was around noon when he dropped her off at the house where her father was waiting for her.

I asked Rueben what he remembered about the trial. The first thought that came to his mind was that this was the first criminal trial in Cottonwood County, and that he was a very important part of this historic event. He said there was a lot of publicity leading up to the day of the trial. The courtroom was packed every day. There were spectators that brought along their lunches so they wouldn't lose their seat when court recessed at noon. He said he was very nervous on the day of his testimony. He'd never even been in a courtroom before, and now he was testifying in a criminal trial. The thought of it gave him an uneasy feeling in the pit of his stomach. He said that once he was on the witness stand, he kept his eyes on the attorney asking the questions and didn't look out at the crowd or the jury, who had their eyes solely focused on him. He said he answered each question honestly and to the best of his recollection.

I asked Rueben what Judge Flinn was like. He remembered the judge was an older guy, who was highly respected and conducted the trial according to courtroom procedures. The attorneys presented themselves in a professional manner. I asked him if he thought the judge did the right thing by dismissing the case. He said, "The jury should have gotten the chance to deliberate the case." He felt the jury probably would have brought in a guilty verdict, but wasn't sure, since he wasn't one of the jurors. Rueben said the people throughout the community were thoroughly disgusted with the verdict because they were quite certain Clarence murdered his wife.

Another interesting thing Rueben shared with me, was that Clarence was known to spend lots of time at the Peavey Elevator in Garvin where he would sit for hours reading books on how to commit the perfect murder. Several months after the trial, Clarence came up to Rueben in a grocery store and said, "You did a good job at the trial." Rueben didn't respond; he just walked away and left the store.

Mr. Anderson shared with me what he remembered about the Larsons. He said Martha was a very kind, hardworking woman. She raised hogs and chickens, always had a huge garden, helped Gilly in the fields during planting and harvesting season, and helped with the chores. She went out of her way to help others. He told me about the time his father was in the hospital for a few days. While he and his mother were away tending to Arvid, Martha walked the short distance to the Andersons' farm, milked the cows, pasteurized the milk, fed and tended the livestock, and then returned home to tend to her own chores. He remembered a little bit about the hired-hand, Gilly. He said Gilly was a heavy-set man with no formal education; he could not read or write and walked with a slight limp, but was soft-spoken, very dependable, and a hard worker. He managed the farm, planted and harvested the crops, and helped Martha with the chores. Gilly lived with the Larsons about a year or so and then moved on, helping other farmers in the area. He wasn't quite sure when or why Gilly left the Larsons' employ. He said Clarence was quite lazy for the most part, and when he went to town, he always dressed up and wore a hat. Rueben described Clarence as a big man who had very large hands. He described Clarence as a "smooth talker." He liked to flirt with the ladies at the coffee shop. Clarence never bothered much about the farm; he left that to his hired hand, his son, and his wife. He told me that before Clarence went off on his hunting trips, Martha loaded the car with a couple of frozen chickens, choice cuts of frozen pork, canned vegetables, and baked goods. Then Clarence would give all this food to Jean and Oliver Sande when he stayed with them during the hunting season.

"Justice was not served for Martha," said Rueben. He felt Clarence should have been found guilty for this terrible crime. Rueben said the Anderson family still owns the Lake Sarah Township property, but the house and other buildings are long gone.

AFTER THE ACQUITTAL

AFTER THE ACQUITTAL, Clarence quickly adjusted to his new-found freedom. Gone were the thoughts of his pathetic life spent in the tiny jail cell with nothing to do from day to day. He probably didn't have many visitors, but maybe Jean stopped by on occasion; we don't know for sure.

Clarence moved back in with Jean Sande in the big house in Tracy. He probably went back to working as a handyman, lining up painting jobs and other fix-it projects in the Tracy area. He continued attending local auctions and estate sales, buying up antiques, restoring them and selling them at a reasonable profit. Clarence appeared to be doing quite well. He also had stashed away the money he received from the sale of his farm shortly after Martha's death, and the money he received in the wrongful death suit.

ANOTHER DEATH IN THE LARSON FAMILY

IT WASN'T LONG before another tragedy struck the Larson family. The following story was found in the *Balaton Press Tribune* newspaper, July 1965.

"In 1965, Ronald and his family were spending July 4th weekend visiting relatives in the Marshall and Balaton areas. At the time, they were living in Omaha, Nebraska and were visiting with a great-grandmother, Mary Harmon of Balaton. A terrible tragedy occurred near the beach at Lake Yankton on July 5 at about 4 p.m. Debra Jean's body was discovered in four feet of water near the 40-foot pier. Efforts by the Balaton Fire Department and Dr. Norman Lee of Tracy failed to revive the child. No one witnessed the incident and the child had been checked minutes before she apparently fell from the dock. She had been wearing a life preserver most of the day but did not have it on at the time of the mishap. The tragic accident shocked the crowded Lake Yankton beach filled with picnickers and swimmers. Ronald and Kolene were on the beach and picnic grounds when the incident occurred.

Funeral services were held at the Zion Lutheran Church south of Balaton with Rev. Holger Hagen officiating. Interment was in the church cemetery. Debra was survived by her three brothers – Ronald, Robert and Donald; grandfather Clarence Larson, grandmother Cenith Uhre and Mrs. Frank Hatton was a great-grandmother. Pallbearers were Norman Strifling, Dennis and Erick Erickson and Gary Garrels."

Martha and Clarence Larson grave stones
(photos by author)

CLARENCE MARRIES JEAN

IT WAS ALMOST three years since Martha's death, before Clarence and Jean married on April 23, 1964 in Pipestone. They set up a joint checking account in the Walnut Grove Bank but did not have a savings account. They shared a safety deposit box, did not have any securities on deposit, and there was no life insurance on Jean or Clarence at that time.

Jean received approximately $250 a month from a disability she sustained in a traffic accident. Clarence also received some money from a disability, bringing the total income to around $347 a month, plus odd jobs in painting and other related lines of work that Clarence picked up during the month so the couple appeared to be doing quite well.

Jean worked for Dr. Workman. She cared for his wife, Cecil, until her death. She continued in his employ as housekeeper and tended his horses located in a barn on a parcel of land at the north end of the Larson property. The two established a close relationship over the years.

Dr. Workman had purchased the parcel of land in September 1948 from Malcom and Evelyn Nash. The doctor kept his horses in the barn on the Larson property, and they took care of them for him. Workman was known to ride his horses in the Box Car Days Parade in Tracy every year. He was an excellent equestrian.

By 1967, Dr. Workman was eighty years old and felt it was time to sell the horse property. On August 1, 1967, Clarence and Jean purchased this parcel of land from Dr. Workman for $2,000 on a warranty deed that stated "a payment of $20 a month until the principal was paid, and no interest shall be paid on the contract." As part of the contract, the Larsons permitted the doctor to keep his horses on the premises, promised to care for them and maintain the building and the property during the entire time of the contract. During the lifetime of the doctor, the Larsons would receive the sum of $20 per month for the care of the horses and maintaining the premises, and this would appear as a monthly credit of $20 on the contract each month. The doctor would pay the property taxes and insurance during his lifetime, but upon his death, if there was a balance due on the principal, the Larsons would assume the responsibility and agree to pay taxes and insurance.

On his personal stationery, Dr. Warner Workman typed up an amendment to the contract on October 21, 1969, which stated, "In consideration of the special services and care given me by Clarence Larson and his wife, Jean Larson, I hereby state that should I die before the obligation assumed by the grantee in the attached contract for deed, I do hereby bequeath the property described as paid in full as of the date of death. In testimony whereof, I hereby set my hand. Signed W.G. Workman" It was notarized by attorney Algyer.

Here is a story about Clarence and Jean from the Tracy Area Headlight Herald *1970s issue that I found quite interesting.*

"In the first week of January 1970, Clarence and Jean received a llama as a gift from a friend, Frank Sharping, of Chamberlain, South Dakota. "Ali Baba" was seven years old and weighed 600 pounds. The llama had once appeared on *The Ed Sullivan Show* and was brought here from an amusement park in New York City. The llama was halter broke and was kept in the barn with Dr. Workman's horses. Llamas come from the Andes mountains of South America and are used to carry an average load of 150 pounds for up to 12 hours a day. The Larsons changed the llama's name to "Lonnie," and it was often one of the attractions in the Box Car Days Celebration."

Dr. Workman died on March 8, 1974. His estate was held in probate court by executors Algyer, Buzzell & LaRocque. Clarence and Jean appeared in probate court in Lyon county on November 25, 1974 to hear the petition for conveyance of property according to the real estate contract with Dr. Workman. The executor of the estate appeared in court. No one appeared to oppose the petition, and attorney Buzzell was authorized to convey the land to the Larsons by probate deed, pursuant to terms of the contract. Final conveyance of the property was recorded at the Office of Register of Deeds at the Lyon county courthouse in Marshall on February 10, 1975. All future tax statements for the property were sent to Clarence and Jean Larson.

Jean and Clarence with Lonnie
(photo from *Tracy Area Headlight Herald*, January 8, 1970)

NEIGHBORS ARE
CONCERNED

IT WAS OCTOBER 1980 when neighbors became concerned that Jean Larson had not been seen by anyone since late September. Several concerned citizens met at the Skandia Café in Tracy to discuss her whereabouts. The group found it disconcerting that nobody had seen her for several weeks, either walking the dog, mowing the lawn, tending the garden, or washing the car. The community suspected that Clarence might have done something to Jean because of the suspicion surrounding the death of his first wife. Neighbors asked Clarence where Jean was, since no one had seen her for quite some time. Clarence told several different stories: Jean went to see a doctor in the Twin Cities concerning her arthritic condition. Jean had gone to Wisconsin and California for health reasons. Jean had gone to Wisconsin to visit a cousin. Jean was gone, and she didn't want anyone to know where she went. Jean had run away with another man.

As best as could be determined, Jean was last seen on October 2 at her ceramics class, and on October 5 at an auction sale, but had not been seen by any other person since that time. Jean drove a four-door Chevrolet, and the whereabouts of the vehicle were unknown at the time. Jean's dog had not been seen playing in the yard since early October.

ANTIQUES AUCTION SALE

CLARENCE AND JEAN loved antiques and spent many hours at auctions and rummage sales, grabbing some great deals. It didn't matter if a piece of furniture was in rough shape, because Clarence could repair just about anything and Jean was an expert at refinishing, so they made a wonderful team. The couple was known to have rummage sales, along with a huge antiques sale at their home in the fall of the year, usually making a pretty good profit.

Richard Riener, a licensed auctioneer from Sleepy Eye, had been in contact with Clarence during the month of September 1980, but at that time, Mr. Larson stated he wished to postpone the auction until later in October so he could obtain more inventory. Riener met with Larson at his residence on October 6, at about 10:30 a.m. and finished up things around 1:30 p.m. Absent from the meeting at that time was Jean. Riener felt it odd that she was not present and asked Clarence where his wife was. He said that her arthritis was giving her a lot of trouble and she left with friends who took her to the Twin Cities. Riener stated that in all other auctions, Jean took an active part, as far as drawing up the auction bill and the pricing of certain antique items going into the sale. Riener said that on that day, Jean's dog was in attendance.

There were always several items in the house that were protected from the sale by Jean. One of the articles was a beautiful china closet that was in the living room. Jean had inherited the china closet from her mother, as well as many of the articles found inside. Mr. Riener remembered the sale of 1979 when he jokingly made the comment that if he could sell the china closet and its contents, he could make them a lot of money. Jean was very emphatic at that time and said that under no circumstances would she sell those articles. This year, in 1980, when the sale time came, the china closet and fancy dishes, as well as collected rare glassware that Jean had protected in the past, were put on the sale bill and ordered sold by Clarence in Jean's absence. Riener indicated his concern about selling her precious items. Clarence told him that they were intending to move to California and start over in another area. Riener still had a strange feeling about the fact that Jean was not present during the drawing of the auction bill.

On October 26, Riener arrived at the Larson residence about an hour before the sale. Again, Riener noticed that Jean was nowhere to be found. He inquired of Clarence as to her whereabouts. Clarence stated that she was not at the sale and that she had already gone south because of her arthritis. Riener knew something was wrong as Jean was always present at all their auctions and took an active part in all the details. Larson was happy with the results of the sale and made a comment later that he wanted Riener to handle the sale of the house for him. However, Larson did not set a date for the proposed sale of the property.

George Quigley, owner-operator of the local garbage service in Tracy, picked up the Larson garbage on October 27, a Monday, which was the normal day for pickup. On October 29 or 30, Clarence called for a special garbage pickup. He was leaving the area and this would be the last pickup; he would gladly pay the extra charge. There were two or three rather heavy black plastic bags at curbside, and Mr. Quigley took them to the area dump the same day. Clarence stood at the end of the driveway and watched Quigley load them into the truck. Later, during the investigation, BCA agents went out to the dumpsite with Quigley to find out where he dumped the trash that day. He showed the agents the area where the Larson trash was dumped. Rumor had it that the agents claimed there was "no money available to excavate the dump." It was reported that the manager of the landfill would not go near that area of the dumpsite ever again because of rumors he heard about Jean's disappearance. The abnormal aspect about this was that Clarence and Jean never used plastic bags for garbage at any other time before this.

Large Antique
Auction

We will sell the following personal property at public auction at our home located at 484 Craig Avenue, on Hwy. 14, Tracy, MN on

Sun., Oct. 26, 12:30 p.m.

ANTIQUE FURNITURE

The Harrand Co. pump organ. ornate top with mirror in very good condition; Buffet with serpent head with a tier above buffet, claw feet; Large china closet with curved glass on sides and flat door on front. very good condition; Secretary desk with curved door on china closet. very good; very old book case; two captain chairs with cane seats. hardwood round table; arm chair with casters, back and arms same height; hardwood buffet. stack book shelf. 3 tier; cabinet with vents. very unusual; two hardwood chests. magazine rack; knick-knack stand with 5 shelves; plus a few other items

ANTIQUE DISHES

Cut glass bowl. numerous depression glass; some Limoges china; six cut glass salt dishes; plates from Austria, Germany, Bavaria, Haviland and Nippon; some Fostoria; three Hull vases, Bavarian. Haviland and unmarked bowls; Hull centerpiece; spoon dish with spoon. numerous vinegar cruets; numerous cup and saucer sets; numerous knick-knacks. set of Meito china, Kobe pattern. not complete. occupied Japan items Royal ruby glassware; plus other dishes and bowls; the above list will consist of approximately 200 items

MISC. ANTIQUE ITEMS

Two Aladdin lamps. glass, wall telephone. complete. two gold ladies watches. chain type. Ansonia mantle clock, very ornate. with alarm. about 60 cylinder type Edison phonograph records; three glass butter churns. porcelain cream tester. oval picture frame. cast iron bank. old Heinz crock bean pot. electric. braided hair watch chain; Waltham watch, 15 jewel adjusted. 8 days. ship watch. plus other pocket watches; **Bowey's root beer wooden barrel with spigots. very sharp;** three penny machines. match. candy and peanut. all working; carnival souvenir horse; collectors moon spoons and holder; collection of Avon and boxes; some souvenir spoons, numerous wheat pennies two seltzer bottles; wall telephone box. kerosene lamps; two sod irons and holder. some crocks and crock jugs. lone wolf picture. ice tongs. wooden hand wringer. scrub boards. 1 wood; two copper boilers. see-thru jewelry box. two cast iron seals. numerous marbles. some cat eyes. copper tea kettle; glass lid fruit jar: cuckoo clock. made in Germany; plus numerous other antique items.

MISC. HOUSEHOLD ITEMS

1847 Roger Bros. setting of 12 silverware. reflection pattern in wooden chest. double bed with wooden headboard, two chest of drawers, vanity with handkerchief drawer on top. night stand. two book shelves. writing desk and chair. two orange vases with clear glass bottoms. Smith Corona typewriter. 20 inch boys bicycle. 3 speed. like new. tricycle. plus a few other items

Clarence and Jean Larsen, owners

Rich Reiner Springfield Dave Bosacker Tracy auctioneer
Citizens State Bank of Walnut Grove MN. clerk

Not responsible for accidents
Terms CASH

Auction Bill
(photo from *Tracy Area Headlight Herald*, October 20, 1980)

CONTACT WITH TRACY POLICE DEPARTMENT

In an effort to find out more about this case, I decided to contact the Tracy Police Department to see if they might have any information about the investigation conducted when Jean disappeared. In January 2018, I called the Tracy Police Department and spoke with Chief Jason Lichty. I introduced myself and explained the nature of my call. He was very interested in my request and told me he would look around for the files. He said he was busy and it might take some time to track this down, but he assured me he would call me back as soon as he had some information. From previous experience in looking for long-lost information, I've found that old stuff tends to get discarded after many years of being in storage, so I guess I was a bit skeptical that I would ever have access to these important records.

Finally, a few weeks later, I received a call from Lichty

informing me that he'd found a box of files in the attic of the police station. This was an amazing discovery for me. I was so happy to hear these records had been found and was eager to get my hands on them. For me, it was like finding a hidden treasure. Just think how excited I was to have the opportunity to go through this dusty old box of records that no one had ever laid eyes upon for almost forty years. The following officer reports, interviews, BCA documents and other information were retrieved from the box. Originally the interviews were tape-recorded, entered into evidence, and held by Agent Berg of the BCA for safe-keeping. The recordings had been transcribed at a later date and placed in the investigation file.

I also contacted Sheriff Wallen at the Lyon County Sheriff's office to search through their files on the case. I did find some interesting information about the case that had not been included in the file at the Tracy Police Department. It has been included within the following information below.

A CALL TO DISPATCH

ALL WAS QUIET at the Tracy Police Department on October 27, 1980, until a call came into dispatch at 8:02 p.m. when Barbara Herder stated she wanted to talk to an officer. Officer Horner was assigned to go to the Herder residence to check things out. He arrived there at 8:17 p.m. and was met by Jerry Herder. Barbara stated that one of her old classmates had called her and said she hadn't heard from her mother for approximately two weeks. Horner asked who the classmate was and Herder said Olivia Zoellner (aka Olivia Sande). Zoellner told her that approximately three weeks ago, Clarence Larson called and told her not to call or write to her mother, Jean because she was gone. Zoellner asked him where she went and Larson told her she took a lot of money and went to Wisconsin. Herder stated that two weeks ago Zoellner called Larson and asked where her mother could be reached. She stated Larson was caught off guard and stated she went to California. Zoellner asked if he had a telephone number or mailing address, to which he stated, "No." The officer left the residence about 8:30 p.m. Later that evening, Horner contacted Officer Lee and explained the situation. He asked Lee to talk to Larson and ask his wife to contact her daughter.

Officer Lee met with Larson the following day at 2:30 p.m. stating that his stepdaughter, Olivia, would like to contact her mother, but she did not know where to reach her. The officer asked him where his wife was. He stated she had helped him prepare for an auction sale he had on October 26 and then went to Wisconsin and on to California. Larson said he did not have an address or telephone number where she could be reached. When asked if he had relatives in California, he replied that he and his wife had relatives in the San Diego area. The officer advised Larson if he were contacted by his wife to have her contact her daughter, either at home or at work. Larson then stated that sometime the following week he intended to go to California to be with his wife. Officer Lee advised Larson to notify the police department before he left and his house would be put on a residential security list while he was gone. Larson said he already had someone lined up to look after the house while he was away. During that contact, Officer Lee was left with the impression that Mr. Larson knew the whereabouts of his wife and was not concerned about her well-being or safety at that time.

Later that day, Lee contacted Zoellner, informing her that Larson stated her mother was in California but that he had no phone number or address. Zoellner said she was not aware of any relatives in that area, but she wasn't very close to her stepfather or her mother lately. She said she last spoke to her mother around October 1, 1980 and had not heard from her since. She said she did not trust her stepfather and feared some harm may have come to her mother.

Zoellner stated Larson had phoned her at work and asked her to phone him that evening. Zoellner said she didn't know what to say when she talked to him. The officer advised her to inquire where Larson was going to meet her mother next week when he went to California. Officer Lee said that her mother was an adult and could travel where she wished, when she wished, without notifying anyone. Lee said that if she heard from her mother, to notify the Tracy Police Department.

At 8 a.m. on October 31, 1980, Clarence walked into the Lyon County Sheriff's office in Marshall and reported to Sheriff Leon Van Den Broeke that his wife, Leona Jean Larson, was missing. Larson stated several times it would not be practical to locate her and return her home, as she would only leave again, but to assist in locating her for knowledge of her whereabouts. He indicated that he did not wish the missing person's report to be broadcast through other police departments in the area as the report would then go to the Tracy Police Department, and they would make more out of it than it was. He further stated that his wife had taken a hefty sum of money when she left and that she was an alcoholic and had been drinking excessively. When asked when his wife was first missing, he stated he heard some noise at approximately 2 a.m. on October 6, and as he slept upstairs and his wife downstairs, he did not check it out. When he awoke that morning, he found her gone and the doors unlocked. On being asked why he waited so long to report her missing, he stated she had left a husband from a former marriage for about eight years before she was located, so he was not alarmed. Clarence stated that he would be leaving to visit his son in Omaha, Nebraska.

Later that day, Sheriff Van Den Broeke spoke with Thomas Healy, Chief of Police at Tracy, and mentioned the missing person's report filed by Clarence Larson. Healy stated that Clarence had contact with the Tracy Police Department on October 27 and again on October 28 in regard to his wife missing. Healy informed the sheriff that he would visit with investigating officers and check with neighbors that might be able to shed some light on Mrs. Larson's disappearance. The sheriff would meet with Healy at a later date for further details of the investigation.

THE INVESTIGATION BEGINS

ON NOVEMBER 2, Chief Healy received a phone call from Olivia Zoellner of Bozeman, Montana. This was the first conversation Healy had with Zoellner. She stated she was the daughter of Jean Larson, and although she and her mother were not extremely close, they did keep in touch, and that her mother was extremely fond of Leslie Jean, Olivia's daughter and Jean's granddaughter. Olivia stated that her stepfather had called her on or about the 10th day of October 1980 and informed Olivia that her mother was not at home and that Olivia should not attempt to phone her mother on her mother's birthday, which was on the 13th of October, since she had headed to Wisconsin to stay with the Zenders, or some name like that. The previous phone contact Olivia had with her mother had been in the latter part of September so that the lapse had only been a couple of weeks, and her mother had not indicated any trip or intention to take a trip.

Olivia was concerned that her mother did not call Leslie Jean on her birthday which was October 25. Her mother always called Leslie Jean on her birthday and sent a gift. Olivia mentioned that her mother had a drinking problem previously, but lately, she had been pretty good. It was at this time that Olivia called Clarence and was told by him that her mother had gone to California to see some friends. Healy told her that the situation was being investigated and that she would be kept informed as time went along.

On November 3, Healy received a call from Zoellner, stating she had received a call from Clarence on November 2. He told her that her mother had run away with someone and had not gone to Wisconsin. Jean had left him and was now gone. He told Olivia that he was at his son's residence in Omaha.

Officer Thomas Thompson and Sheriff Van Den Broeke went to Tracy on November 5, to meet with Tracy Police Chief Thomas Healy in regard to the "missing person" status of Jean Larson. At that time Chief Healy provided numerous additions to the case file, which came from various persons that he had interviewed regarding this incident.

On November 6, Thompson discussed the case with BCA Agent Michael O'Gorman and furnished him a copy of the report to date. Then Thompson called Redwood Sheriff Jerry Luttman and requested him to check with the Walnut Grove Bank for any possible business transactions involving Jean Larson.

PHONE INTERVIEW

AT 4:30 P.M. on November 6, Thompson called Clarence at his son's residence in Omaha. The call was made on a Lyon County Sheriff's Office recorded line. Below is the conversation that took place. It appeared that Clarence was not concerned at all with his wife's disappearance and made negative comments about her. (CL = Clarence Larson; TT = Thomas Thompson)

CL: Hello.

TT: Hello, Clarence.

CL: Ya.

TT: This is the sheriff's office in Marshall.

CL: Yes.

TT: We're just checking if you've heard anything?

CL: Van Den Broeke?

TT: No, this is Thompson.

CL: Thompson.

TT: Ya.

CL: No, I haven't.

TT: Ok, any ideas?

CL: No.

TT: Where she could have went to.

CL: No idea.

TT: Oh, ok, I tried calling you at home, I thought maybe you'd be back by now but no answer.

CL: Pardon.

TT: I said I tried calling your home but no answer so.

CL: I'm down at my son's now.

TT: Ok, I have this number that you gave Leon.

CL: Ya.

TT: Ok, what have you heard?

CL: Well, you got to do more. I tried to stop her from drinking and the hell with the whole business.

TT: Um-hm.

CL: And she took off in the night.

TT: Um-hm.

CL: So, I think she's alright, but I think she will show up.

TT: Um-hm, um-hm.

CL: I'm sure she'll show up again.

TT: Um-hm.

CL: But I had a problem with her drinking. I had her in the hospital you know and 5 or 6 times in the hospital and I had her in ah, Rush City with the doctor and ah, peritonitis; bad, they tapped almost a gallon and a half of (inaudible) but ah, I ain't going to worry about it.

TT: Um-hm.

CL: I just felt that I would, ah, see if you could run it on the teletype there.

TT: Um-hm, where do you think she could've gone to?

CL: I have no idea.

TT: Um-hm.

TT: Has she ever done this before with you?

CL: No, no.

TT: Um-hm.

CL: Done it with her second husband.

TT: Um-hm, when was that?

CL: I'm her third one.

TT: You are?

CL: Ya.

TT: How long you been married to her?

CL: Since ah, 1964.

TT: How long you going to be down there?

CL: Oh, I might be here a month or so.

TT: Ok.

CL: So, you got the telephone number.

TT: Ya, if you hear something, give us a call.

CL: Ya, I'm sure she'll show up, I ain't worried about it.

TT: Um-hm.

CL: You know--

TT: Ya, ya.

TT: Do you think she'll go out to her daughter's?

CL: I doubt it, they weren't getting along either.

TT: Um-hm.

CL: No, has Olivia called?

TT: No, she hasn't, no.

CL: Ya, if I hear anything, I'll drop you a line or a call.

TT: Ok.

CL: I'm out here painting on a house now. I'm dry, I'm losing my voice I guess.

TT: Ya.

CL: Ya, well thanks for calling and if I hear anything, I'll give you a buzz.

TT: Ok.

CL: But I'm sure she'll show up within ah, oh, I don't know how long a time

TT: Um-hm, um-hm.

CL: But ah, she's a stubborn old shit.

TT: Ya, ya.

CL: And she is about 1/16th Indian blood in her and the God-damn liquor doesn't do her any good, you know.

TT: Um-hm, that will do it.

CL: God-damn it, been a battle with the damn stuff.

TT: Um-hm.

CL: So, thanks for calling, if I hear anything, I'll call you.

TT: Ok, you do that, take care.

CL: Thank you now.

TT: Goodbye.

Sheriff Luttman called Thompson on November 7 with the following information that he'd requested the day before: "Clarence and Jean Larson had a checking account in the Walnut Grove Bank. They did not have a savings account. The last check that Jean wrote out was to Mary's Ceramics, dated September 30, 1980. Clarence still had some checks coming through. On October 26, 1980, Clarence Larson had an Auction Sale and the Walnut Grove Bank clerked the sale. Jean Larson was not around on the day of the sale."

The above information was obtained by Deputy Couyer from the bank president, Ron Keil.

Later that afternoon, Thompson called Clarence's number at his Tracy residence and the operator informed him that the number had been disconnected at the request of the resident.

Then Thompson placed a call to Doctor Norman Lee at Rush City during the first part of November. The doctor stated that he had both Clarence and Jean Larson as patients while he had his office in Tracy. Agents O'Gorman and Berg arrived at the Rush City Clinic for the purpose of executing a search warrant for Jean's medical records. The doctor immediately gave them all information contained in the files. He stated that they should check the medical records at the Tracy Hospital as there would be x-ray records on file for Jean at that facility. Dr. Lee stated that Jean was examined in 1974 for some fractures due to a supposed car accident. There were also x-rays on file at the Mankato Orthopedic Clinic where she was referred to a Dr. Lippman for examination. Dr. Lee stated his last contact with Jean was in 1977 at which time she was confined as a result of an ulcerated sore on her leg and an enlarged liver. She had a large amount of fluid in and around the liver area and it was possible that she could have died at that time. Due to proper treatment given at the time, Jean did in fact survive the medical problem. She had much blood work done then and supplied us with the extensive serology report.

Dr. Lee stated that he had a fairly good rapport with Mr. Larson, however he did recall one incident in which Mr. Larson came to Dr. Lee's residence demanding money for the care of a horse Dr. Lee boarded at the Workman barn. He stated that Mr. Larson was quite emphatic that money was owed to him for the care of that horse, which was not the case. Dr. Lee stated his wife was very apprehensive of having Mr. Larson around, due to his abusive nature at that time.

Thompson decided to contact Jean's daughter to find out the last time she had spoken with her mother. The officer telephoned Olivia on the evening of November 7 at her home in Montana. This is a summary of that conversation.

Olivia stated that the last time she spoke to her mother was on September 21. Jean told Olivia that she was making something for her granddaughter who would be eight years old on October 25. Jean was very fond of the child and never forgot her birthday. Olivia knew her mother never traveled because she never wanted to leave her personal things in the house alone. The last time Olivia saw her mother was the summer of 1979, and she had a good relationship with her mother. Her mother had a drinking problem, but it wasn't as bad as it used to be. Olivia never got along very well with her stepfather. Olivia left home when she was seventeen or eighteen years old. Her mother and Clarence had been together off and on since she was six years old. Olivia felt her mother stayed with Clarence out of fear more than anything else. Clarence called Olivia about October 10 and stated that her mother had left with someone by the name of Zenders and they went to the Twin Cities. Clarence told Olivia that Jean was also going to California to visit someone. When Olivia asked him who she might see there, Clarence replied, "No one in particular." Clarence called her on October 31 and told her that he had reported her mother missing to the sheriff. Jean's first husband, Oliver Sande, lived at Chisholm, Minnesota but Olivia didn't think she would contact him, as he still had hard feelings over their divorce many years ago. The only allergy Jean had was hay fever in the spring and the fall. Whenever Olivia would call Clarence asking about her mother, he would get upset and have to think before he answered her.

BCA GETS INVOLVED

ON NOVEMBER 10, Robert Berg, Bureau of Criminal Apprehension (BCA) agent spoke with Agent Michael O'Gorman, who was advised that on November 5, he (Berg) spoke with Sheriff Leon Van Den Broeke and Chief Deputy Thomas Thompson at Marshall. Van Den Broeke and Deputy Thompson discovered some inconsistencies in the disappearance of Jean Larson and their impression at that time was that there may have been foul play involved in her disappearance. Two days later, on November 12, Chief Thompson requested that the Bureau become involved with the investigation. Bureau agents were briefed about the investigation thus far. Berg was provided with copies of all reports compiled by Lyon County Sheriff's office and the Tracy Police Department and they were made a portion of the report. Also provided by Thompson was a list of individuals that they had contacted thus far, and a list of individuals to be contacted in the future.

INVESTIGATION
INTERVIEWS

CHIEF HEALY AND agents of the Bureau of Criminal Apprehension conducted an intensive investigation including interviews with approximately thirty friends, relatives, and acquaintances of Jean Larson concerning her whereabouts. Below are some excerpts from transcribed testimonies from those who were interviewed. This gives the reader a personal look into the intimate relationship between Clarence and Jean, their personalities, the family dynamics, and how others viewed the couple's life together. What happened to Jean remains a mystery to this day.

On November 13, 1980, agents Robert Berg and Michael O'Gorman of the BCA and Chief Deputy Thomas Thompson, Lyon County Sheriff's Department interviewed Mary Lou DeBlieck, owner and operator of Mary's Ceramics in Tracy. The interview took place at the Tracy Municipal Building, and the following information was obtained.

Mary Lou DeBlieck first became acquainted with Jean Larson around June 27, 1980 when she had come to the ceramics shop located in the basement of her residence. Since that time, Jean had become an avid customer and had been at the shop every day that it was open, Monday through Friday. She considered herself to be a fairly close friend of Jean's. DeBlieck never heard Jean say anything derogatory about her husband and had the impression they had a good marital relationship. During one of their conversations, Jean said that if anything happened to her husband, that she had her mother's house she could move into (location unknown). Jean talked about her dog and pet hamster frequently and mentioned that because of the dog, they were unable to go any place for any length of time. DeBlieck stated the last time she had seen Jean was on or about October 2, at the ceramics shop. She felt it odd that Jean had not returned to the shop, as she was making several items as gifts for friends and family for Christmas, and was working on a salt-and-pepper shaker set as a birthday present for Diane Deming. Jean had special-ordered several items that she had not picked up yet and DeBlieck felt Jean would have notified her if she was planning a trip.

DeBlieck stated that on October 6, Clarence Larson called her and told her that Jean had gone to the Cities and that she would not be down to the shop. DeBlieck received another call from Larson on October 25, stating that Jean had gone to California because of her allergies and that she would not be back. Later that day, Larson arrived at the shop, picked up Jean's items, and paid DeBlieck for the unpaid portion of Jean's bill. During that contact, Larson told DeBlieck that he was thinking about selling everything, including the house, and going to California to visit his wife. He also made the statement that he "may be back alone." Another incident that took place that day was that after Larson paid the bill, he stated that he had $80 worth of slips at home yet. DeBlieck said that Jean always kept the paid receipts for the ceramics supplies and items that she had gotten, in her purse and she thought it rather strange that Jean would have taken the receipts out of her purse prior to leaving on a trip.

There was another thing to mention. "Jean did tell me she was redoing furniture and that's why her fingernails were dark, but the day Clarence came over and paid the bill, he made the statement to me, he said that she had this allergy and that her fingernails were turning dark from it; I thought it was kinda funny when he said that."

DeBlieck indicated that she had heard Jean had a drinking problem, but she had never seen her intoxicated, and felt that if she were an alcoholic, she would not be able to have done the quality of work she was doing in the ceramics class. DeBlieck stated that Jean complained that the cold bothered her. She had pain in her hands and legs due to arthritis, but DeBlieck was unaware of any other health problems Jean might have had. She made it clear that Jean would never leave her dog or hamster at home. If she planned a long trip, she'd take them with her.

It was on November 13 that Diane Deming was interviewed. Agents Berg, O'Gorman, and Thompson conducted an extensive interview as they learned that Diane was Jean's closest friend. The interview was held at the Tracy Municipal Building.

Diane Deming indicated that she worked afternoons at the Williams Westside Grocery Store in Tracy, and that she had known Jean for approximately two years. During that time, she and Jean had become very good friends and confidantes and advised that she probably knew Jean better than anyone in the Tracy area. According to Deming, during the conversations she had with Jean, she got the impression that Mr. and Mrs. Larson did not get along too well, specifically, she stated that Jean would complain about Clarence going to auction sales and bringing stuff home for her to refinish, and that she did not like Clarence's children by the previous marriage; they were lazy, and she expressed the opinion that she thought they were taking advantage of both Clarence and her. Deming stated that on several occasions while she was at the Larson residence, Jean would make some derogatory remark about her husband and that her dog would then start barking at Clarence. According to Deming, there was no obvious animosity between the two of them; they seemed to tolerate each other well, and Deming never saw them argue or run down each other in front of other people.

Typically, Deming said that Jean would arrive at the Westside Store around 12:30 p.m. or 1:00. Prior to Jean's becoming involved with ceramics, she would spend approximately two to three hours at the grocery store with Deming and consume two to five, seven-ounce 3.2 Miller beers. However, since she had started going to ceramics class, she would arrive at the Westside Store around 12:30 and stay until about 1:00 p.m. and then go to the ceramics class. While she was at the store, Jean would have one or two seven-ounce Miller beers, but during the last week, prior to her disappearance, she had a cold and was drinking Orange Crush pop rather than beer. She would show up three or four times during the week, but never came by on Fridays because this was the day Clarence would go to auction sales in Walnut Grove.

Many times, she would take an eight-pack of Miller beer home with her. But the last time Deming was in the Larson residence and happened to look in the refrigerator, there were about four or five of these Miller eight-packs in there untouched. Deming didn't think Jean drank that much, never saw her intoxicated, and didn't feel she was an alcoholic.

Deming said that Jean became involved with ceramics in the spring of 1980. She was very involved with it and went every day when the shop was open. She had several projects started that were going to be given as Christmas gifts, and it was very unusual that she would leave without completing the projects. She was also getting ready for the antiques auction sale in October and Deming was supposed to help with the sale.

Jean expressed to Deming that she would like to take a trip to see her daughter in Montana, but there was no mention as to when she was planning the trip. Deming was of the opinion that Jean was not going anywhere during the winter and if she were planning a trip, she would certainly have informed Deming of it. The Larsons had no friends or relatives in Minneapolis, St. Paul, Wisconsin or California. There was a stepson in Nebraska and a stepdaughter in Texas somewhere. Jean's mother lived in northern Minnesota but she was deceased. Deming found out that Jean's first husband was killed in the war, but did not know the husband's name.

(Note: Jean was not being completely honest with Diane, at the time, because Jean's first husband, Walter Kronman, died in 1978). Jean divorced the second husband who was living in northern Minnesota, and the third husband was Clarence.

Deming said the last time she saw Jean was during the week of October 1; she had talked to her on October 2 by phone when Jean asked her if she wanted to go to an auction sale. Deming was sick at the time and did not attend the sale with her. On or about October 8, Deming had talked to Clarence and he told her that Jean had gone to Wisconsin and then on to California for her arthritis. Deming thought this was extremely strange, because during one of their conversations, Jean made the comment that "California was one of the dumbest places to go for arthritis because of the high humidity."

Deming spoke with Clarence on October 25 and asked her if she would help with the sale, and be there between 8:30 and 9:00. "He asked me what I drank with my vodka, and I asked him why, and he said he thought we'd have a few snorts after the sale. And I told my husband he's callin' him the next morning and tellin' him I have the flu; cuz I'm not going." This was the last contact she had with Clarence.

Deming was asked if she knew of any physical violence that may have occurred in the marriage. "Jean always told me if her and Clarence ever got in a fight that she'd kick him home, cuz she had a temper." She said, "My eyes were coal black and he just knows, I'm part Indian, so he'd know." But she never said anything about hittin' or throwin' things or anything like that.

Deming made the following remarks – "If they're lookin' for her, she does wear a wig, and when she doesn't have her wig on, she looks totally different than what she does when she's got her wig on. I wasn't even thinkin' about that until I read the description in the Tracy paper, and that doesn't fit her either. Her normal hair was grayish, about shoulder length and in the summer, she would often wear it tied back."

Deming stated they had separate bedrooms upstairs but Jean preferred to sleep on the davenport downstairs. She never said why they had separate bedrooms.

Deming gave a description of Jean – she was 5' tall, weighed about 95 pounds, with graying shoulder length hair, which was extremely thin. Most of the time, she wore a dark-colored wig. Jean had a scar on the inner portion of her lower right leg and she had a pin in her right ankle which was the result of a fracture which occurred a long time ago. She had a scar over the left eye. She wore a partial plate and her dentist was Dr. Hyland from Tracy. Jean also wore reading glasses.

Deming felt it was extremely strange that Jean would have taken off without telling her about it. Deming was familiar with the usual clothing Jean wore, and if she could go through the remaining clothes in the house, she would be able to tell whether Jean left voluntarily or not, by the clothes that were left in her closet.

I was interested in interviewing Diane, now years later, to see what she remembered about her good friend, Jean, and her thoughts about what might have happened to her. I spoke with several people in the Tracy area that knew Diane well to see if I could make contact with her. A friend of Diane's gave me her telephone number. I contacted her to set up an appointment for an interview.

I met Diane at her home on January 17, 2018, not

knowing what to expect. Discussing what happened to her dear friend might be an emotional experience for the both of us. When I arrived, we visited for a bit, then had coffee and cookies.

Diane took me back to the days when she first met Jean at the William's Westside Grocery Store where she worked in the afternoons. She had known Jean for about two years before her disappearance. She described Jean as a nice, friendly, quiet lady. They became very close friends. Diane felt that if Jean planned on going on a trip or leaving for an extended period of time, she would have told her. Diane said, when she didn't hear from Jean, she had the feeling that Clarence had done something to her.

Diane did not feel that Jean drank a lot. She said Jean would come into the store two or three times a week and drink one or two 7 oz. Miller beers. But since she had become involved with her ceramics class, she did not spend that much time in the store anymore.

Diane described the first time that Jean invited her to the house. Jean showed her around the home and pointed out all of her beautiful antiques. She had a large spoon collection that Jean said she would never part with. At that time, Jean had a German Shepherd dog named Lola. One day while Diane was visiting Jean, Clarence drove up the driveway. Jean blurted out, "here comes old fuckhead." Lola growled and barked. The dog hated him.

Diane talked about the auction sale and how Clarence called her a couple days before the sale, informing her that Jean had gone out of town. He asked her if she would help with the sale, and also asked her what she liked to drink because they would have a couple snorts after the sale. Diane said she did not want to be around Clarence without Jean there. Diane had her husband call Clarence on the morning of the sale to tell him she was sick. Diane said Clarence was very mad at her for not helping with the sale.

Diane said that one day, investigators met with her to show her a woman's shoe that was found somewhere near the Tracy area. They thought it might be Jean's. The size was 8 or 9, but Diane said, Jean wore a size 5.

Diane remembered being in Jean's bedroom upstairs after her disappearance. Investigators had her look in the closet to view what was left of Jean's clothing. Diane noticed Jean's bed was gone; the room was bare. She looked in the closet and saw only three tops left that were Jean's; they were all her favorites. Diane said if Jean left on her own, she would have taken the three tops that she always wore.

Diane said Jean would never leave her dog and hamster. If she intended on being gone for a long time, she would take them with her; she loved her animals.

Diane felt that Clarence murdered Jean and disposed of her body somewhere.

Diane has many fond memories of her dear friend and still thinks of her often. She hopes Jean will be found someday.

At 11:45 a.m. on November 14, Agent Berg contacted Olivia Zoellner by telephone. During the tape-recorded conversation, the following information was obtained.

Olivia Zoellner stated that the last time she spoke with her mother was on September 21, 1980, when she called her, and nothing seemed out of the ordinary. The first indication that something might be wrong was when Larson called

Zoellner around October 13, advising her not to call on her mother's birthday, as she had gone to Wisconsin for a couple weeks to visit some friends. Zoellner stated that she thought it was somewhat strange at the time because her mother had made no mention of going anywhere, in their previous conversations.

When the birthday present for her daughter did not arrive on October 25, she became even more concerned, because during the September 21 telephone conversation with her mother, Jean had mentioned the present she was making for her granddaughter. Jean never missed sending a present to her granddaughter and would also call her on her birthday. Due to the fact that the present had not arrived and her mother had not called on her granddaughter's birthday, she became even more concerned and placed a call to the Larson residence. Clarence seemed to be very nervous and evasive about the questions put to him by her. Clarence advised Olivia that after going to Wisconsin, Jean had gone on to California, but did not know where she could be reached. At this time, Zoellner called Barb Herder in Tracy, requesting that she attempt to locate Jean's whereabouts.

The next contact Zoellner had with Larson was around the first or second of November advising her that he was at his son's residence in Omaha. At that time, Clarence stated that he had reported his wife missing and told Zoellner that Jean had run away with someone else.

Zoellner stated that the marital relationship between her mother and step-father appeared to be fine, on the surface, but there were underlying problems within the marriage. There was no physical violence between the couple that she was aware of, but they did argue a lot. When she was living with her mother and stepfather, her mother did have a drinking problem, but she felt her mother's drinking problem had improved considerably within the past few years. Her mother did have a touch of arthritis but it was not a major problem.

On November 17, Agents Berg and O'Gorman were advised by Chief Healy that he had received information over the weekend from Zoellner that she had additional information she wanted to tell them. At 9:45 a.m., Agent Berg placed a call to Zoellner. Again, the conversation was recorded.

Zoellner told Berg that she received a call from Larson on Friday, November 14. He wanted to know if she made any plans for coming home for Thanksgiving or Christmas, and she told him she had not planned to do so. Larson said he would send money for them to make the trip. She said this was the one and only time that she can ever recall of Larson offering to send them money for any purpose. Larson wanted them to come out for a visit when her daughter was out of school, but Zoellner said she did not have the vacation time or the money to do so.

Zoellner gave some background information about her father. His name was Oliver Sande; he lived in Chisholm and was between sixty-four and sixty-five years of age. He was a retired mine worker from the Chisholm area. She stated that whoever interviewed her father would find that Sande was still rather bitter about the divorce from his wife. Larson met her father when he would come to northern Minnesota to hunt, and she did not know any more than that.

Zoellner was asked about the last name of Zender that her mother might have known. But she did not recall any friends of her mother's from the Twin Cities area by the name of Zender.

O'Gorman inquired about some articles that were listed on the auction bill which were believed to be family heirlooms. Zoellner informed the agent that her mother wanted her to have the china closet and the articles within it. On Zoellner's last visit to Minnesota, her mother tried to get her to take the items home with her, as she feared for their safety in and about the house. But all of these items went up for sale on October 26.

Agents Berg and O'Gorman were informed that at the time of Larson's first wife's demise, he lived in Murray County near the Lake Sara area. At that time, he was farming, and it was believed that there were still buildings standing on the land that Mr. Larson had once owned.

In an attempt to locate that property, agent Berg contacted Orville Muck, Murray County Sheriff on November 17. Sheriff Muck stated that he knew the property but did not believe there was a house left on it; however, there were several outbuildings still standing on the property. The sheriff made arrangements to take the agents to the property, after first getting permission from the current owner to set foot on the premises. Once they got out to the farm site, they noticed two buildings still standing, but these were in rough shape.

While standing at the location, the sheriff relayed information concerning an incident involving his daughter, Marlys Hegstad, who had been a roommate of Clarence's daughter, Janet, while attending college. The sheriff happened to run into Clarence in September or early October 1980. Clarence gave Orville a copy of the auction bill, indicating the antiques auction at his residence on October 26. At that time, Clarence asked about Orville's daughter, Marlys, and wanted to know where she was currently living. Since Marlys and Janet were roommates at one time, Orville saw nothing wrong with the request and told Clarence where his daughter lived.

A brief time later, Orville spoke with his daughter by phone, at which time she indicated that Larson had showed up at her residence. During that visit, Larson was acting in a rather strange and peculiar manner. While Larson was on her property, he took ten to twelve photographs of her in and about her residence. She also stated that he was a very "touchy" person, running his hands on her body and touching her numerous times. Since his conduct was rather offensive in nature, she became somewhat concerned for her safety. Larson also commented that his wife was not of good health, and due to her arthritic condition, was unable to leave the house much anymore. Hegstad did not want anything to do with Larson and did not intend to let him back onto her property.

Hegstad had a second run-in with Larson at an antiques sale she attended. At that sale, Larson again came up to her and tried to strike up a conversation. Larson noticed she had made several purchases and offered to haul her property home for her. Hegstad declined the offer. Later she found out that certain articles of her purchases had, in fact, been picked up by Larson and placed in his car, with the intent to deliver them to Hegstad's residence. Hegstad removed the packages from Larson's car and placed them in her vehicle, as she did not want Larson on her property.

OTHERS INTERVIEWED

MORE INTERVIEWS WERE conducted on November 13 and 14 by BCA agents Robert Berg and Michael O'Gorman, and Chief Deputy Thomas Thompson, Lyon County Sheriff's Department at the Tracy Municipal Building in Tracy.

Mary Deal was the next-door neighbor and had known the couple since 1973 when she moved into the house. She said the Larsons kept to themselves and seemed to be pleasant; she never heard any arguing or saw any physical violence. Deal stayed away from Clarence because of the background involving the death of his first wife. Deal knew Clarence was a painter by trade and that the couple bought and sold antiques. They had a large antiques auction once a year. The last one was held on October 26, 1980.

Roy Deal knew Clarence since 1973 when he and his wife, Mary, moved into the house next door. Clarence seemed pleasant but was somewhat "different," but Deal could not give any details. Deal only spoke with Clarence six or seven times and kept his distance because of stories he heard about his first wife's death. He never knew of any marital problems but recalled one incident that stuck out in his mind. Deal stated in late September or early October, he was at the Larson home and Ford Ankrum, a local contractor, and Clarence were installing new water pipes. Mr. Ankrum asked Clarence to have his wife turn on the water to check for leaks. Clarence said, "We're not speaking." Deal stated the last time he saw Jean was about a month and a half previously when she was outside doing some yard work. He last saw Clarence at the antiques sale on October 26. Deal thought it was strange that Jean was not there that day, as she had a great interest in antiques and should have been at the sale. But his son, Ronald, from Nebraska was there, and that was the first time he ever met him. Mr. Deal said that Clarence was very friendly with Cora Peterson. Deal knew that Jean drove a 1971 brown Chevy that Dr. Workman had given her.

David Bosacker assisted Rich Reiner at the auction on October 26. The gross receipts for this sale were approximately $8,000 and around the same amount in 1979. Besides the antiques business, Clarence was known as a self-employed painter. He only knew the Larsons on professional terms; he did not socialize with them. One time while he was at the residence and looking at antiques, Larson took him to an upstairs bedroom and showed him 8 or 9 antique guns that were kept under a mattress. David never knew Jean to have a drinking problem but saw both of them drinking in his presence. On the day of the sale, Clarence told David that his wife had gone to the cities and later they planned to travel to California for the winter because of her arthritis. David asked Clarence if he wanted him to mention Jean's absence at the sale and Clarence said he didn't want this made known. David noticed that Ronald, Clarence's son, was at the sale helping out. David said the Larsons owned two cars—one was a station wagon used for Clarence's paint business and the other, a 1971 Chevrolet driven by Jean. He last saw Jean several months previously. Bosacker stated that the gals at the Red Rooster restaurant didn't care for Clarence because he always came in and wanted to touch them, and they didn't like that.

Lyle Peterson was a self-employed building contractor in Tracy. Clarence contacted him on October 18 or 19. Mr. Larson said, "I'm going south for a couple of months." Clarence informed Lyle that William Koch would watch the house and if there were any problems, such as broken windows, etc. that Koch would contact Lyle to correct the problem. Clarence would settle with Peterson when he returned. Peterson assumed that Clarence and Jean were going together. The couple kept to themselves and did not socialize much. Peterson said, "The only time I ever known Clarence to be laid up is when he stuck his finger in the fan in the bakery and flipped the end of it off."

At about 7:10 p.m. on November 13, Lyle Peterson returned to the Tracy Police Department advising them that he had received a telephone call from Larson and thought that they should be made aware of the information he obtained. Larson had called Peterson, asking if everything was okay at the house. He told Larson everything was fine and that he had not heard from Bill Koch about any problems. Larson informed Peterson that Koch was not doing the job and he wanted Peterson to take over the responsibilities of looking after the house and correcting any problems that might arise. Larson told Peterson to check the house every day, and on two or three occasions told him not to let anyone know that he had a key for the house. At no time did Larson ever mention anything about his wife, but did say he planned on leaving Nebraska and going to his daughter's residence in Texas.

Gordon Johnston stated that he had known Clarence Larson for about thirty years and had known Jean for twenty years. Johnston was an insurance agent. He stated that on October 30, 1980, Mr. Larson entered his insurance office for the purpose of having some personal business copied. Larson advised him that he was leaving town and was going to Omaha and then on to California. He didn't recall whether Larson mentioned his wife going with him or not, but he assumed that they were going together and that they would be back sometime in the spring. He stated that the Larsons had no insurance policies with him and he did not know who they may have insurance with.

Wayne Wiese, a neighbor since 1977, spoke only briefly to Clarence six or seven times. Wiese last saw Jean mowing the lawn on October 5. Jean's dog always barked at him when he left for work in the morning, but since the early part of October, Wiese had not seen or heard the dog when he left for work. Wiese said the only thing unusual at the Larson residence was an old trailer parked right in the middle of the driveway between the house and the horse barn. Wiese said he never paid much attention to it and didn't remember seeing it parked there before.

Arlen Thomas worked with Clarence for about twelve years and was employed off and on as a handyman. Clarence seemed even-tempered and he never saw him angry. Thomas never heard of any marital problems, and the couple did not socialize much. The last time he saw Jean was about a month and a half previously when he helped Clarence move a desk into the basement to be refinished. At that time, there was no mention of Jean going anywhere.

Cora Peterson had known the Larsons since 1971, when she lived next door. Jean would come over just about every day, sometimes three or four times a day. She would have the llama and her dogs with her. They had horses and chickens, too. Jean was a very interesting person. Peterson had since moved away and did not see Jean quite as much. Jean would complain to her about Clarence being so lazy at times. Her last contact with Jean was during the week of September 15, 1980, when they had a telephone conversation. During the week of October 6, she called the Larson residence, and Clarence said Jean was gone. Clarence stated that Jean did not like him telling people where she had gone or when she would be back. Peterson said she spoke to Larson just prior to the auction sale, asking if Jean was back, and he said that his wife couldn't take the cold and that she had left and that he had no idea when she would be back. Peterson then called Larson after the sale and was told by Larson that he had hired someone to take care of the sale, as Jean couldn't stand to be out in the cold weather. He also stated that he was planning on going to a warmer climate and that they planned on traveling a little bit.

Peterson advised that during this conversation Larson seemed to become upset and used obscene and vulgar language, which she stated she had never heard him use before. She said that she had never known Jean to leave for any extended period of time without telling anyone where she was going and that she felt it was odd that Jean would leave just prior to the auction sale. She felt that Jean had money saved from when she worked for Mr. and Mrs. Workman for over seventeen years, so if she did in fact happen to pick up and leave, she would have plenty of money to live elsewhere; plus she inherited all her mother's personal property when she died. This was mostly antique furniture and appliances, which was eventually sold off at their auctions. She said Jean was very attached to her pet dog and the hamster, and she would never go anywhere without taking the two animals with her; she just loved them so much.

Jack Chambers knew Larson for about ten years. He, Larson, and several other men would meet at Skandia Café around 6:00 every morning for coffee. The topic of conversation was general in nature, talking about the weather, what was happening in town, etc. Larson never talked about his family life in front of the group, and there was never any mention of any marital difficulties. Larson had acted strange for the last month or so, and seemed different. Larson had mentioned to members of the group that he was upset with Chambers, and accused him of fooling around with his wife. Chambers indicated that there was absolutely no basis for this allegation— that he had known Jean for only about two years, and that he had been at the Larson residence on two or three occasions, delivering firewood. Chambers would see Jean at rummage and auction sales and would talk to her, but there was no romantic involvement between the two of them. Chambers said he heard from people in town, "Clarence was going to get the skin on the end of my nose, and he was gonna shoot me." Chambers had talked to Clarence two weeks before the auction sale, at which time he had been advised that Jean had gone to the hospital in the Cities and that when she got well, she was going to Wisconsin and from there she was going to Indiana. Clarence said he didn't know what the medical problem was or how long she was going to be gone.

Ford Ankrum was a plumber who repaired water lines at the Larson residence over the past two to three years. He did repair work on the Larson water line running from the street into the house. The Larsons had considerable trouble with the water main running into the house with the pipes breaking, and on several occasions, he had been at the Larson residence digging up that line to make repairs. During the summer of 1980, he had been there on two or three occasions, with the last time being sometime around the end of September or the first of October, the exact date was unknown. He advised that the water line at that time was rerouted from the west side of the house to run from a point located along the north side of Craig Avenue, across the front yard, to a point adjacent to a window located on the southeast side of the Larson house. According to Ankrum, the last time he was at the house, the trench for the laying of the new water pipe was opened and closed the same day. He stated that because of the rerouting of the water pipe, Larson had knocked a hole approximately three inches in diameter in the basement of the house to accept the new water line coming in. He further stated that on the last visit to the Larson residence, that as far as he could recall, Mrs. Larson was not around. Ankrum stated that during his contacts with Larson, he seemed to be a nice enough fellow, but he described him as being somewhat strange. He did not elaborate on this statement. He did not know Mrs. Larson well enough to form any opinion about her.

Janet Larson first heard of her stepmother's disappearance during early October 1980 when she received a call from her father. Clarence advised her that her stepmother left in the middle of the night and Jean had yelled upstairs that she was leaving and would not be back. Janet said, "My father said he slipped his pants on and by the time he got downstairs, she was gone. He said somebody was waiting for her because he saw them drive away." She last spoke with her stepmother on September 14, and Jean never mentioned going any place. Janet stated she had visited her father and stepmother for three weeks in 1979. At that time, she noticed that her stepmother drank quite a bit and she'd smoke cigarettes down the basement and blow the smoke into the furnace because Clarence didn't like her smoking. Janet said she planned on going home for Christmas, but since her stepmother wasn't there, she made plans to visit her brother in Omaha instead. Janet discussed her marital problems with her stepmother and the fact that her husband never gave her any money of her own. At that time, Jean stated she had money stashed away that nobody knew about. Janet did not know how much or where the money was kept. Janet hadn't seen or heard from her since that time and doesn't know where she went. But Janet felt her stepmother had planned to leave for a very long time and had saved up plenty of money. Janet didn't have much to base this on, but it was just a feeling.

Linda Hohler was part-owner of the Skandia Café, which had been purchased in 1979. She said Kathleen Hohler was her sister-in-law. She had known Clarence Larson for about ten years. She had gotten to know him quite well, as he would stop in for coffee every morning. Clarence very seldom discussed his personal life with anyone. Hohler felt Clarence was a very strange man. The women around the café did not like him very well, inasmuch as they were aware of the background involving the death of his first wife, and also due to the fact that he would attempt to hug them or pat them on the back. Because of this, Hohler and the other girls in the café attempted to stay away from him as much as possible. Hohler stated she last saw Larson a couple days after his sale. He came in the café one morning, took a look at the round table and never sat there, which was a little unusual, because he always sat there. Instead, he sat at the counter, ordered a cup of coffee, had about two swallows of it, and then got up and left. And that was the last time she saw him. Hohler described the time Larson called one of the waitresses. "I think he said, hello, sweetheart or honey or something like that. And then he kind of laughed. And she recognized the laugh and she hung up on him." The word on the street was that Clarence had asked the waitress' mother when the waitress was working, if she was working on a Saturday night, what time she got done, what time she came to work, those kinds of things. Hohler said none of them wanted to be around him alone, and they always kept the back door locked.

Kathleen Hohler was part-owner of the Skandia Café. Hohler first met Jean during the summer of 1980 while attending ceramics classes at Mary's Ceramics Shop. Hohler remembered one conversation with Jean when she said that if she ever had to leave Clarence, she had a house somewhere that she could go to. Hohler indicated that she had no idea where this house was located. She said Jean told her they had separate bedrooms, but there was no indication there were problems in the marriage. She felt it was extremely strange that Jean would take off without completing her ceramics projects that she intended to give to friends and relatives as Christmas gifts.

She stated that in recent weeks, Clarence had been acting somewhat strange. On October 30, he came into the restaurant for coffee; rather than join the usual group at the round table, he sat at the counter, ordered a cup of coffee, turned around and glared at the group of men, then got up and left the establishment. Hohler talked about another incident that took place sometime around the first of October; Clarence came into the café one morning and was sitting there; then when he went to leave, he came through the kitchen and said, "I'll kill that son-of-a-bitch." Hohler asked him what he was talking about, and he said that Chambers was at the Larson residence and had gotten fresh with Jean. Another incident—on the Saturday before the sale, Gordon Johnston, the insurance agent, was in the café and Clarence came in and sat beside him and they talked for quite some time, just the two of them. That was the first time anybody had seen Gordon with Clarence.

Gary Retzlaff indicated that he was the Larsons' paper-boy and that the last time he had seen Mrs. Larson was on September 20, 1980, at which time she had paid him for the newspaper. He stated that he frequently saw Mrs. Larson; however, he did not have much to do with Mr. Larson. On the days that he delivered papers, when Mrs. Larson was there, she would invite him in for a cookie or a piece of candy. On the days Mrs. Larson was not around, he would find a piece of candy in the mailbox where he would place the newspaper. He stated that because of the newspaper strike which lasted September 13 through October 6, he had not been at the Larson residence. After the paper strike ended, he started delivering papers but had not seen Mrs. Larson, nor had there been any cookies or candies in the mailbox. He would usually hear the dog bark when he delivered the paper, but since October 6, he had not heard the dog. Retzlaff stated that on or about October 21, he received a call from Mr. Larson stating that he wanted to stop the paper, as he was going to California and would not be back until spring.

William Koch used to run a gas station in Tracy, where Mr. Larson did business; however, since his retirement, he had no personal contact with the Larsons. He had known Mr. Larson for many years and had known Mrs. Larson since their marriage. Koch stated that on or about October 25, he was approached by Mr. Larson and asked to watch the house while he was gone for the winter months. According to Koch, Mr. Larson advised him that he was going to his son's place for an undetermined amount of time. Koch stated that he flatly refused to watch Larsons' place and advised him that he wanted nothing to do with the deal. Two weeks before the

VICTIMS OF FOUL PLAY

auction sale, Koch had a conversation with Larson, at which time he was advised that Jean had gone to California and that she would not be back for the sale. Koch had no idea where Mrs. Larson might have gone.

Janet Cyr stated that she, along with Jean and a couple other ladies, would attend rummage and auction sales throughout the area. Cyr said during conversations with Jean, she got the impression that Mr. and Mrs. Larson did not get along too well; she ran down her husband in front of the other girls and stated that she ran the household and that if Clarence didn't like it, he could move out. Mrs. Larson made it clear that she bought the house and she owned the house, and said, "I rule the roost in this house and what I say goes." One day, they were having coffee and Clarence pulled up and all Jean said was "Here comes fuckhead," and the dog started barking, and every time she said that, the dog would bark.

In front of people, Jean would be nice to Clarence, but behind his back, talking to the girls, she would really run him down. Cyr said that Clarence would do the dishes or whatever Jean needed done because the house was Jean's and he knew it. If things didn't go right, Jean said, "He can leave." Cyr was asked if she had the impression that Jean might have something over Clarence, other than the house. Cyr said, "Not really; Jean never said that he ever hurt her." Cyr said, "One day I was at the door and I don't remember what was said, but he stood there and I was outside and he said, 'Oh, I've never hurt anybody in my life; I never have.'"

Jean was getting sick and tired of her husband going to auction sales and bringing antiques home for her to refinish.

Jean could spot a dish that was antique. She bought a dish for 65 cents at a rummage sale that was probably worth about $300; she knew her antiques. Cyr knew Jean drank beer but did not feel she was an alcoholic. Jean loved her dog and would not go anywhere without her dog and hamster. Cyr called the Larson residence in early October asking for Jean to see if she wanted to go to a Tupperware party. Mr. Larson advised her that his wife had gone to the Cities but there was no mention as to why she had gone or when she would be back.

Judy Hanson, along with Jean and a couple of other ladies, would attend rummage sales throughout the area, and they had coffee at the Larson residence on several occasions. Hanson got the impression that Mr. and Mrs. Larson did not get along very well, with Jean specifically stating that "she could live without him and that she wore the pants in the family." Hanson last saw Mrs. Larson around September 26, when they were at a rummage sale together. Hanson spoke to Mr. Larson on October 7 to see if Jean was still planning on coming to the Tupperware party. Larson said his wife had gone to the Cities and did not indicate when she would be home. Hanson said that she sold Avon products and that sometime since Mrs. Larson's disappearance, she had called the Larson residence to have him pick up Mrs. Larson's Avon products that she had ordered. He arrived at the Hanson residence later that day and said his wife had gone to California. Hanson said he smelled of liquor and seemed to be "drifty." Hanson stated that Mrs. Larson never gave any indication she was planning a trip or going anywhere.

Faye Hatch owned the property near the Larson residence, which was the old dairy building. Hatch had known the Larsons for thirty-five years. Hatch said the first thing that struck her as being odd was that one day in early October she noticed the garage doors were down, and the garage doors were usually never closed. The shades were all pulled down and the shades were never pulled down like that. So, Hatch walked over to her building and on her way there, she peeked into a window of the Larsons' garage and it was absolutely empty of a lot of things that used to be in there and the car was not there. Hatch had never known Jean to just pack up and take off before. The last time Hatch saw Clarence was at his auction sale in late October.

Lucille Larson was married to Roy Larson, brother of Clarence; she had known Clarence all her life and known Jean for fifteen to twenty years. Lucille stated that Jean's mother had died and all the property she inherited at the time of her mother's death had been sold. Lucille said she did not know of any property Clarence and Jean owned, other than the house in Tracy. Lucille was unaware of any friends or relatives the Larsons had in Minneapolis, Wisconsin, or California. The last time Lucille had seen Jean was at the Curtie-Kasa auction sale in Garvin on October 5. Clarence and Jean came out to their residence for lunch, then went to the sale in Garvin. At that time, there was no mention of either Mr. or Mrs. Larson planning a trip. Lucille first learned Jean was gone when she called the Larson residence on October 13 to wish Jean a happy birthday. Clarence told her Jean had gone to Wisconsin to visit a cousin, but there was no mention as to when she left nor when she would be back. Lucille stated that Clarence did not tell either her or Roy that he was leaving town, but had called Mrs. Janice Larson, whose husband was George, advising them he was leaving. Lucille said that Jean had arthritis in her hands and legs, but did not feel that it was much of a problem, stating Jean seemed to tolerate it fairly well. She knew Jean drank beer but never saw her intoxicated. Lucille stated that Jean would never leave her dog and hamster behind; she loved the animals.

Mr. and Mrs. George Larson George stated that he was Clarence's nephew and had very little contact with Clarence and Jean over the past several years. George stated that he was farming Clarence's property at the time of Martha's death. George stated the last time he had seen Jean was several months ago and at that time she did not mention she was planning a trip.

Janice Larson, George's wife, stated she had known Clarence and Jean for the last several years but did not consider herself close to either one of them. The last time she saw Jean was on October 5 at Roy Larson's residence, and she had talked to them for just a couple minutes prior to going to the auction sale in Garvin. At that time, there was no mention of either Clarence or Jean going anyplace for the winter. A few days before the auction sale of October 26, Clarence called Janice and asked her to help him with the sale. On the day of the sale, she was advised that Jean had gone to Wisconsin and that from Wisconsin she was going someplace out west because of her arthritis problems. At that time there was no mention of Clarence going to Nebraska, and Clarence told her that shortly after the first of November that he was going

VICTIMS OF FOUL PLAY

to close up the house and go out west to meet Jean.

On the day of the sale, Clarence pointed out several cut-glass items and told her that they belonged to Jean's parents and grandparents, and that they were nearly 100 years old. There was no mention as to why he was selling all of the antique items that belonged to Jean. They had no idea where Jean had gone or any knowledge of relatives or friends in Minneapolis, Wisconsin, or California.

Oliver Sande was interviewed by BCA agents at his home in Chisholm on November 20, 1980. Here we get some more background information on Jean and her family life. This was a lengthy interview, and most of it is included here.

Sande said they were married on Good Friday, April 3, 1941 at Forest Lake. "We were living at St. Croix Falls at the time, and I was partner with Jason Miller at the Dallas House. We lived together until she took off in 1951 or 1952. Olivia was born in 1946 and the twins, Jennifer and Jeffrey, were born in July 1949. I think Jean left in 1951 because the twins were two years old at that time. She took Olivia with her, who was five years old then."

"She left, and cleaned out the house, took everything that wasn't too hot or too heavy, like the refrigerator and the stove and the washer and the dryer, but everything else was gone. She left the twins in their beds, in their cribs until my mother-in-law, a day or so later got a hold of me and told me to come and get my twins before they freeze to death. Jean was gone."

Sande said he was not aware Jean was going to leave him at that time. He stated they had just seen the judge because

Jean was going to file for divorce or something.

"It was in November 1951, around hunting season; Clarence came up here with his truck and they cleaned out the whole setup. I raised the twins; my mother took care of Jeffrey and my sister took care of Jennifer, who was mentally retarded now, from the abuse she got from her mother."

"There finally was a divorce just before the statute of limitations of seven years. I was served papers in June or July and I told my attorney I'll go down there, to Pipestone, where Jean was at the time. Jean wanted $20,000 and $1,000 a month. That was a huge amount of money, and the place wasn't worth one half of that or maybe not even a quarter, and $1,000 a month was impossible to make for anybody. My attorney, Vic Holstrand, arranged to have it go through the attorneys. The divorce was final in early December 1959, but I had to borrow and mortgage the home again to get $5,000 to pay her off. Vic sent the money down to Pipestone to settle the divorce."

"The last time I spoke to Jean was at her father's funeral. I wanted to ask her where Olivia was, and she pushed the kid aside and said, 'I don't want to talk to you.'"

Sande talked about Walter Kronman, Jean's first husband. He had known Kronman all his life. He said Kronman had died of a heart attack in April 1978. He attended the funeral. It had been rumored that Kronman had died as a result of a hunting accident, but there was no truth to that whatsoever, according to Sande.

Sande was asked how he met Clarence. He said that Jean and the neighbor woman, whose husband was in the army, would go to the tavern and they met these deer hunters from down around Tracy and Garvin, and got to know them.

VICTIMS OF FOUL PLAY

"Then one time Jean brought Clarence home and introduced me to him. Clarence would come up here fishing too. Then I got to know people in the Revere area and I'd go pheasant hunting down there. Then we'd visit the Larsons during pheasant hunting season: me, Jean, and Olivia. And sometimes Martha would come up here with Clarence and the kids. I knew Clarence about two years maybe, off and on, but I never knew him personally, how he was or anything."

Sande talked about the Stillings family; Jean had so many uncles on her father's side. The Stillings family was a very elegant family. Their father was good people. Frank Stillings had six brothers in WWI and they had enough land out there, out at Valley City, North Dakota; they owned sections and sections. Jean's mother was originally from Wisconsin. And Jean's grandmother, at eighty-five, "was still shackin' up with guys." That's the kind of family she came from. And Belle, Jean's mother, was just the same thing; like mother, like daughter. "Grams", Belle's mother, was married four times. Sande did not know any relatives in Minneapolis, Wisconsin, or California, nor did he know any people by the name of Zender.

"At the time, I worked three jobs and when I'd come home, her and her mother would fight like a son-of-a-gun. One time I came home, it was my birthday on the 4th of July; here she was sittin' on the steps with a handful of hair in her kimono, and she says, 'You son of a bitch, if you ever take my mother anyplace, I'll leave.'"

"'Well,' I said, 'what's wrong?' Oh, we had a down-and-drug-out fight. Well, her mother caught her with this Eddie Loco and tried to straighten her out. She was half goofed up, and that's when they got in the fight. They were both scratched to hell and said that I beat up on 'em. I wasn't even around; I was workin'. I picked up Belle when I see her walkin', the poor woman, and I took her to the grocery store, and then she told me what happened. And then later on when they got to be friends again, they blamed the fight on me."

Sande talked about how he took care of the kids and raised them. Jennifer was in the University Hospital for forty days because of the abuse by her mother, Jean. She was two years old at the time. She had peritonitis. Jean was feeding Jennifer too much baby food, of just pumpkin and carrots.

On November 17, Agent Supervisor Robert Rysavy read an earlier investigation report filed in 1962 that revealed Clarence over insured, or highly insured his wife Martha, who perished in a suspicious farm accident. Agent O'Gorman contacted Bill Quinn, a representative of The Insurance Crime Prevention Institute (ICPI) in Chicago, IL. Mr. Quinn stated that unless a claim had been filed, their agency would not be able to investigate further. Quinn would check his records for an insurance policy on Martha and Jean and advise what he found at a later date; however, it appeared no follow-up was done on this matter.

Officer Daniels had a telephone conversation with Dr. Bicek, a veterinarian in Tracy, on November 18. He said that on September 27, Mr. and Mrs. Larson brought in their dog, Loah, to be vaccinated for the parvo virus. This disease required another vaccination two weeks later. On October 11, Clarence brought in the dog for the second vaccination. The dog was a basset hound, a very short, fat dog. The dog was a spayed female, gold and white in color and about nine years old. Neighbors had not seen the dog for quite some time, and Dr. Bicek stated that he had not put this dog to sleep. The officer checked with other veterinarians in Tracy and none of them had any record of putting this dog to sleep.

SEARCH WARRANT ISSUED

THOMAS THOMPSON APPLIED for a search warrant for the
Larson home. On November 18, 1980, Lyon County Court
Judge George Marshall signed the warrant. The following
areas of the premises were to be searched: a white, two and
one-half story, wood frame house and a white, wood frame,
oblong structure utilized as a garage, located approximately
500 feet north of the residence. This warrant was extremely
specific, searching for items belonging to or used by Jean,
such as: "personal letters to or from friends, relatives, or business associates, personal diary, financial records (i.e. phone
or utility bills), personal checkbook, personal phonebook,
articles of personal clothing or the lack thereof, personal effects, such as jewelry, toilet items and the like or the lack
thereof, personal luggage or the lack thereof, a dog or the lack
thereof, a 1961 Pontiac station wagon, six-passenger Safari,
MN license #AWM-136, a black wig or the lack thereof."

A second search warrant was issued on November 20. The following items were taken into custody and are listed as follows: "carpet samples from living room, carpet sample from entryway between dining and kitchen rooms, various samples of a red substance thought to be blood from kitchen walls and cupboards, bath towel-green in color, one pillow case, one bedsheet, one handkerchief, one green jacket thought to be female." As a result of that search warrant, blood stains were found on three walls in the kitchen. Samples were taken and sent to the BCA laboratory for further testing.

AGENTS TRAVEL
TO OMAHA

WITH THE INVESTIGATION stymied for leads in Tracy and other parts of Lyon County, Agents O'Gorman and Berg and Sheriff Van Den Broeke decided it was time to make contact with Clarence Larson, who was staying at his son's place in Omaha. On November 24, they traveled to Omaha and contacted the Omaha Police Department, Homicide Division, to advise them of their purpose in the area.

They met with Detective Larry Roberts to review the information on the case. Agents O'Gorman and Berg felt that Jean Larson disappeared on October 6, which in all probability was the date she was murdered. The removal of her body from the residence could be easily accomplished with the attached garage situation, and her body most likely had been disposed of somewhere in Minnesota.

Roberts prepared a search warrant for the search of the

1971 four-door Chevrolet registered to Jean Larson. The purpose of the search warrant was to search the vehicle for blood stains, human hair samples (grey and brown in color), a woman's medium-length black wig, and one woman's purse containing personal identification of Jean Larson.

On November 25, Officer Lenker and Sheriff Van Den Broeke drove to Ronald Larson's residence in Omaha and served the search warrant to Linda Larson, Ronald's wife. A complete search was made of the vehicle and no evidence was found. It was noted that the trunk of the vehicle was cluttered with various painting items, two shotguns, shotgun shells, handgun shells, a scoop shovel, and miscellaneous items.

Detective Clyde Nutsch telephoned Clarence Larson at his son's residence on November 25. He agreed to come to the Omaha Police Department for an interview. Larson was transported to that location by Detective Larry Lenker and Agent Robert Berg.

The interview commenced at approximately 2:00 p.m. with Agent Berg, Agent O'Gorman, and Sheriff Van Den Broeke in attendance. Larson was asked what information he could supply regarding the disappearance of his wife and he related the following information.

He stated that recently his wife had been having a problem with drinking. His wife would consume approximately sixteen bottles of beer a day, she slept downstairs and did most of her drinking during the evening hours. She drank after he went to bed in an upstairs bedroom. Larson commented several times that he believed someone was sneaking in the front door of his home at night, supplying his wife with hard liquor. He had nothing to base this on, nor had he ever caught anyone doing this; however, he stated that her level of intoxication on some evenings was greater than if she was just drinking beer. Jean drank Miller High Life. Many mornings Jean was crabby and difficult to be around due to her heavy drinking the night before.

Larson stated he last saw his wife on the evening of October 5. They ate supper around 6 p.m. He went to bed at 8:30 p.m. In the early morning hours of October 6, Jean yelled upstairs, "I'm leaving you, you son-of-a-bitch, and my daughter also." Clarence went downstairs and found that the front door was not standing open but was left unlocked. He thought Jean left through that door. Clarence could not think of any arguments they had on October 5, but he remembered they attended a sale in Garvin that day.

Clarence said he had several conversations with Jean concerning her drinking, and about two days prior to October 5, he had a conversation with her concerning committing her to an alcohol treatment program for her condition. He said he had been in contact with Olivia, and she had gone along with the commitment of her mother due to her drinking problem.

Clarence stated Jean took an unspecified quantity of clothing with her. She carried the clothing in two suitcases—one was gray in color and made from composition board; the second case was blue in color and had a smooth finish. Clarence attributed their marital problems to Jean's excessive use of alcohol. He was not sure where Jean might have gone or what means of transportation she may have used.

Clarence and Jean had separate bedrooms. He suspected that Jean was seeing other men earlier in their marriage but

VICTIMS OF FOUL PLAY

had no indication of anything of this nature going on recently. Larson was aware that Jean was putting money away secretly. He estimated the amount to be around $500 to $600.

The Larsons had a joint checking account, and both he and Jean would carry checkbooks. Jean would have her checkbook with her. Clarence stated two or three times that he did not believe Jean would write any checks but rather would be spending her own cash money which she had been hoarding for a period of time. They shared a safe deposit box at the Walnut Grove Bank and each had a key. Neither he nor Jean had any securities on deposit with any banks, and there was no insurance in Jean's name at that time.

Clarence was asked what friends or relatives Jean might visit. He stated that Jean had an uncle, Elmer Burke, who lived in a nursing home in Chisholm and an aunt, Elsie Burke, who also lived in Chisholm. Jean's daughter, Olivia Zoellner, lived in Bozeman, Montana. There was a second daughter, Jennifer Sande, who was mentally retarded and resided at the state hospital in Brainerd, Minnesota. She had a son, Jeffrey, who resided with his father, Oliver, in Chisholm, and her ex-husband Oliver Sande in Chisholm. Jean's mother and father, Frank Stillings and his wife, Belle, were both deceased.

Larson was asked about the antiques sale on October 26. He said that his son had come up approximately one week prior to the sale to give him a hand with organizing and preparing for the sale. Clarence was questioned as to some of the items that were sold at the auction—specifically, the china cabinet and the items in it that her daughter, Olivia, was to inherit upon Jean's death. Clarence stated that Olivia was on the "outs" with her mother, and Jean was not leaving her anything as was stated in Jean's "will." When asked why Jean's bed and other furniture went on sale, Clarence again stated that this was Jean's idea; she wanted the property sold so that she would not have to worry about it when they moved south. When asked what became of the organ that was on the auction bill, Clarence said that it did not sell at the auction, and that he had given it to his son. Ron transported it to Omaha, and it remains in his house.

Clarence was asked about the replacement of some carpeting in front of the kitchen sink. He indicated that a section of carpet in front of the kitchen sink had been replaced by his wife approximately a week before her disappearance. He explained that the reason the carpet was replaced was that his wife had dropped a bottle of molasses while removing it from the kitchen sink drawer and that it had broken. He said that because she was unable to get the molasses out of the carpet, that she replaced it with a new section that was left over when they had originally installed the carpet.

Larson was advised that Agents O'Gorman and Berg found blood splatter in various places in the kitchen and around the sink area. Clarence said that two days before her disappearance, Jean had cut her hand while opening a fruit jar. It was explained to Clarence that in the areas of the residence where they found this blood, it would be impossible for the blood to be deposited there from a cut hand. Clarence's only reply to this challenge was a simple "Oh."

Clarence was asked what means of transportation he used to come to Omaha. He stated that he came in a 1971 Chevrolet belonging and registered to Jean. Clarence was asked what would happen if Jean would come home, how would she be able to move about or how would she be able to

VICTIMS OF FOUL PLAY

contact him. He stated that he had a conversation with Jean earlier that fall, indicating that after the sale, he was going to go to his son's residence and Jean could reach him there.

Agent O'Gorman requested Larson let them examine the 1971 Chevrolet belonging to his wife and that was parked at his son's residence. Larson had no objection to the request and turned over the keys to Sheriff Van Den Broeke. At that time, Larson was informed that they had a search warrant to search the vehicle.

Larson intended to remain at his son's residence for some time and then drive to his daughter, Janet's residence in Arlington, Texas. Larson stated he had no idea where his wife might have gone and did not seem concerned about her disappearance. He stated that if she was found, he did not want her apprehended; rather, he merely wanted to know where she was so that he could go to her and try to convince her to either come home or check in to an alcohol treatment program. At one point in the interview, Larson referred to the fact that "Jean will show up again," and stated again later, that "Jean will surface again someday."

Agents O'Gorman and Berg were uncertain as to what degree of cooperation they would receive from Larson, so the interview was recorded without Larson's knowledge. The interview lasted about two hours, was later transcribed and became a part of the final report.

Ronald Larson, Clarence's son, was interviewed by phone on November 26 at his place of employment and the following information was obtained.

He stated that he first learned of his stepmother's disappearance on or about October 12, when he received a phone call from his father stating that Jean had left in the middle of the night. He thought she might have gone to Wisconsin or California to visit friends. His father requested his assistance in the upcoming auction sale. Ron stated he was aware of his stepmother's drinking problem and knew they did not get along too well, and because of that, he was not surprised or suspicious when he had heard that Jean had taken off. Ron had seen his stepmother twice during the late summer and early fall of 1980 but was unsure of the exact dates. During those visits, Ron had seen Jean intoxicated and knew she drank beer but did not know if she drank hard liquor. In a conversation with his father about a year previously, Clarence mentioned that Jean should seek professional help with her alcohol problem, but it never went any further than that.

Ron had seen a "will" that his stepmother had drawn up, in which Olivia had been written out of the "will" and was to receive no inheritance at the time of Jean's death. Ron didn't know if this "will" was still in effect, and the last he knew, the "will" was placed in a safety deposit box at the Citizen's State Bank in Walnut Grove.

Ron was asked about any guns that his father might own. As far as he knew, his father owned two shotguns and a .22-caliber pistol. Ron had several antique guns he had left with his father, but Clarence had brought these weapons back to Omaha sometime prior to Jean's disappearance.

Ron advised that after his father was interviewed by Agents Berg and O'Gorman at the Omaha Police Department, he attempted to talk with his father about the disappearance of

Jean, but his father did not wish to discuss the matter and wanted to avoid the issue.

∽◦∼

Olivia Zoellner Agent Berg telephoned Olivia on November 28, to follow up on some things that were discussed with Clarence during his interview on November 25.

Zoellner said that at no time had she discussed with her stepfather about committing her mother to an alcohol treatment program and felt her mother would never have gone along with it anyway. "She would stand up and fight it." She'd never agree to an alcohol treatment program, said Zoellner.

In one of the last conversations with her mother, she told her about her divorce and her mother was quite accepting of it, but "Clarence tried to tell me she was really upset about it, but if she was, she would have let me know. One of the times I had called him to find out just what was going on, where my mother was; he came back at me, that my mother was just really upset at me because of this divorce and that he was really gonna be upset because I was causing him all these problems now."

During the last two or three years, her relationship with her mother had improved, and there were no hard feelings toward her by her mother. Olivia knew nothing about a "will," and as far as she knew, the antiques and china closet were still supposed to go to her upon her mother's death. In August 1979, while I was back there for a visit, "Mom said she wanted to come out, see an attorney, and get a lot of things changed. She never elaborated on it, and I never pushed her about it, so I don't know what she was talking about at the time, but she planned on bringing the dog along, too. But for her to take a trip would have been a big thing. She didn't want to leave the house because she had so much stuff in there that was Grandma's and she was afraid if she left, the stuff would be gone."

When she spoke with her mother, there was never any mention of any cash being saved by her. She told her mother that if she would come to Montana that she (Olivia) would pay for half the trip. From the tone of that conversation, Zoellner had the impression that her mother had no cash saved up whatsoever.

THE SEARCH CONTINUES

ON NOVEMBER 29, Agent Berg, along with officers from the Lyon County Sheriff's office, the Tracy Police Department, and the Minnesota Department of Conservation conducted a search of the immediate area around Tracy for any traces of Jean. Acting upon the premise that Jean may have left her residence on or about October 6, in an intoxicated state, and that she may have succumbed to an accidental or intentional death, it was decided to make a search limited to an area approximately six-to-eight-mile radius of the city of Tracy.

The search party did an extensive search of drainage ditches, valleys, and creeks adjacent to these roads. Abandoned farm sites were also searched. The Conservation Department's aircraft, piloted by Conservation Officer Rich Stotman, conducted the aerial search. The area was full of potholes and wooded areas and these places were frequented by deer, pheasant, and duck hunters. If a body were lying in the open during the hunting season, it would have been reported by this time.

ANOTHER SEARCH WARRANT

ON DECEMBER 2, Agents Berg and O'Gorman, along with members of the MN Bureau of Criminal Apprehension and the Lyon County Sheriff's Department executed another search warrant at the Larson residence. During the initial search of the Larson residence on November 20, Agents Berg and O'Gorman had observed what appeared to be blood spatter on several surfaces within the kitchen area. Portions of these apparent blood spatters were secured by Agents Berg and O'Gorman and subsequently transported to the BCA Laboratory, where they were examined by Analyst Terry Laber, who determined that these apparent blood spatters were, in fact, human blood. The ABO blood type at that time was unknown.

The purpose of the December 2 search warrant was to enter the Larson residence with members of the BCA

Laboratory to do a more complete analysis and interpretation of those blood spatters observed on November 20.

During the execution of that warrant, the following items were seized.

Item #1 - a sample of carpeting, 5" x 6", removed from the southeast corner of the kitchen floor with apparent blood stains on same. **Item #2** - several small pieces of what appeared to be paint chips or plaster chips removed from the southeast corner of the kitchen floor near carpeted area. **Item #3** - a sample of kitchen carpeting, 4" x 32", removed from the lip below the kitchen sink. This is the first piece of carpeting north of the south wall. **Item #4** - one sample of kitchen carpeting measuring 4" x 32", removed from the lower lip below the kitchen sink. This is the second piece of carpeting north of the south wall. **Item #5** - one sample of kitchen carpeting, 3" x 16", removed from lower lip below kitchen sink. This is the third piece north of the south wall. **Item #6** - front drawer panel removed from lower right-hand corner of kitchen sink with apparent blood stains on face and body edge of same. **Item #7** - one strand of hair, grayish in color, removed from the lower left-hand door of kitchen sink. **Item #8** - two strands of hair removed from the lower left-hand door of the kitchen sink. **Item #9** - two strands of hair removed from the lower left-hand corner of the left-hand sink door. **Item #10** - one piece of apparent paint chip or plaster chip removed from the top of a knife rack located to the left and above the kitchen sink. **Item #11** - sample of carpet from fifth step from top of stairway leading to basement with blood stains on same. **Item #12** - one pillow and pillowcase with blood stains on same found in upstairs southeast bedroom on bed. **Item #13** - one knife rack containing six knives with apparent blood stains and tissue adhering to them. Removed from the east kitchen wall above the kitchen sink. **Item #14** - several hair curlers with brown and gray strands of hair attached to same recovered from front living room of Larson residence to be used for comparison purposes. **Item #15** - several strands of brown and gray hair recovered from the southeast lower corner of the south kitchen wall. **Item #16** - several strands of brown and gray hair recovered from mop board on lower southeast corner of the south kitchen wall. **Item #17** - one plastic box containing sample of blood spatter found under the front lip of kitchen sink. **Item #18** - one plastic box containing blood samples from south kitchen wall. **Item #19** - one drawer with blood stains on same removed from lower cabinet area along the north wall of the kitchen. **Item #20** - one door panel with blood stains on same removed from left side of sink assembly. **Item #21** - one door panel with blood stains on same removed from right side of center kitchen sink assembly.

All the above items were tagged and retained in the custody of Terry Laber for transportation to the BCA Laboratory at St. Paul, Minnesota for analysis. Due to additional items found with apparent blood stains that were not included in the original search warrant of December 2, another search warrant was obtained for the seizure of hair samples, knife rack holder, and the seizure of door panels and drawers within the kitchen area, and hair curlers from the living room. That warrant was issued to Chief Deputy Thomas Thompson and signed by Judge Marshall of the Lyon County Court on December 3, 1980.

In searching the kitchen area, blood spatters were observed along the surfaces of the south wall. The blood spatters were below table-top height, were relatively numerous in number but small in size. By shining a high-intensity light along the south wall, investigators determined that the wall above the height of the kitchen table may have been wiped or washed, because above this level, the wall was free from dust; however, below this level, there appeared to be a collection of dust on the surface of the wall.

There were numerous blood spatters along the entire front surface of the kitchen sink, including the right-hand drawers, the center and left doors. The blood spatters on the left side of the kitchen sink appeared to be angular in nature and emanated from the south. Blood spatters were found under the lip of the sink. This would have to have originated from an area lower than sink-top height. Blood spatters were also observed on the front surfaces of the wooden cupboards directly to the left of the kitchen sink and appeared to be angular in nature and emanated from the south.

Blood spatters were observed on the venetian blinds and upper cabinet area directly to the left of the kitchen sink, and appeared to be angular in direction and to have emanated from the area directly in front of the kitchen sink.

Located on the end of the upper cabinet above the sink was a knife rack containing six knives. Numerous blood spatters were observed around the area of the knife rack and there was a small piece of what appeared to be tissue with brownish-colored hair embedded in same.

On the upper portion of the two center sink doors, it appeared as though an attempt may have been made to wipe these clean, as there were visible streaks running down the face of the doors, and when Analyst Laber conducted a benzidine test for the presence of blood in these streaks, he

VICTIMS OF FOUL PLAY

received a positive result.

Cupboards located along the north wall revealed blood spatters on the lower level. Spatters adjacent to the cupboards along the east wall of the kitchen appear to have struck the surfaces at a perpendicular angle, becoming more angular in direction as one progressed westward along the north wall.

A blood spot about 3" in diameter was found in the southeast corner of the floor, directly in front of the right sink drawers. There was evidence of blood spatters found in and about a 4" section of carpeting running along a vertical strip the entire length of the kitchen sink. Other small blood spatters were found in the kitchen carpeting in the area directly in front of the kitchen sink; however, a 24" x 19" section of carpeting which was placed directly in front of the kitchen sink contained no evidence of blood spatters. Examining the remainder of the kitchen carpeting, there was no evidence of blood spatters found in any area other than that in front of the kitchen sink.

Brown and gray-colored hair strands were observed and seized from the front door panels of the kitchen sink. Also seized were several pieces of paint or plaster chips. One piece of paint or plaster chips were seized from the top of the knife rack located above and to the left of the kitchen sink.

The only other areas where blood was found were on a pillow and pillowcase in the upper southeast bedroom (Clarence's bedroom) and on a step leading to the basement area.

On December 2, Laber and Enzenauer conducted a Luminol test on a limited area of the kitchen carpeting and the center front door panels of the kitchen sink. The Luminol test was a preliminary chemical test used to detect the presence of blood on various surfaces. Laber was unfamiliar with the testing procedure, but he reviewed the literature and was willing to attempt the procedure. The test was conducted according to the instructions; however, the results obtained seemed contradictory to the instructions and were inconclusive. No interpretations could be made from this test.

As a side note—just think how DNA and other forensic testing has improved since 1980, and how much more accurate new procedures are in this field. Back in 1980 they were still using the Luminol test to check for blood on surfaces, which was often inconclusive or inaccurate.

During the examination of the basement, an area on the south basement foundation wall measuring approximately 4' x 3 ½' and circular in design was observed to be of a different color and texture from the surrounding area. It had been determined that this was the area in which a new water line had been run into the Larson house on or about the first of October 1980. Ford Ankrum assisted Larson in running this new water line into the house, and he was requested to come to the Larson residence to determine whether the new concrete had been laid at that time. Ankrum arrived on December 3 at 10:15 a.m. and took a close look at the area in question. According to Ankrum, Larson had a 1 ½" galvanized pipe driven through the wall extending for approximately 6" to 8" from the outer foundation and that the new water line was fed through this pipe into the house. Ankrum could not recall whether the new concrete work had been done at that time or not. Ankrum said that the foundation wall was approximately 12" to 14" thick.

On December 3, Analyst Laber, who was an expert in the

VICTIMS OF FOUL PLAY

interpretation of blood spattering, attempted to determine the point of origin of the blood spattering observed in the kitchen area. Through measuring the length and width of the blood spattering, Laber was able to determine the angle at which they struck the surfaces and that from the shape of the splattering, he was able to determine which direction they came from. Incorporating these two factors and through use of string, he was able to project a line back to the point of origin. By connecting several different blood spattering, he was able to tentatively identify the point of origin as being from a point approximately 14" east of the kitchen sink, 35" north of the south wall and 12" plus or minus 6" up from the kitchen floor. Laber stated that from the blood spattering observed; three or four separate blows were struck to formulate the blood pattern.

During the interview with Clarence Larson on November 25, 1980, he indicated that the section of carpet in front of the kitchen sink had been replaced by his wife about a week before her disappearance. He said that the reason the carpet was replaced was because his wife had dropped a bottle of molasses while removing it from the center portion of the sink and that it had broken. Because she was unable to get the molasses out of the carpet, she replaced it with a new section that they had left over from when they originally laid the carpet.

When agents examined the kitchen carpeting on December 2 and 3, there was no indication of molasses being spilled on the carpet in the area adjacent to where this piece had been replaced. Also, in searching the kitchen cupboards on December 2 and 3, two bottles of partially used molasses were found in the cupboard above and to the left of the kitchen sink. Clarence explained that the blood spattering on the wall may have been a result of his wife cutting her hand on a mason jar approximately two days to a week prior to her disappearance. According to Laber, he felt the blood spattering in the kitchen area was not consistent with this type of injury.

EXCAVATING THE PROPERTY

CONTINUING WITH THE investigation, local officials felt it was necessary to do a comprehensive search of the grounds surrounding the Larson residence to see what might be discovered. On December 16, a search warrant was issued to search for the body of Jean Larson at the Craig property, along with any blunt instrument used as a possible weapon, and to be able to utilize mechanized and nonmechanized digging devises to dig dirt to a depth of eight feet and to the interior of the south basement wall in the areas stated in the warrant.

Excavations of portions of the Larson property included digging along the west and south sides of the house where the old waterlines had been dug up and replaced just prior to Jean's disappearance. The State Bureau of Criminal Apprehension, county sheriff's office, and Tracy Police Department cooperated in the effort.

The trench on the south side of the house, approximately 30 feet long and 3 feet wide, was excavated to a depth of 4 feet. No evidence was found in the trench.

A circular area, approximately 15 to 20 feet wide, located on the west side of the property, was excavated to a depth of 4 feet with nothing found in that location either. The trenches were filled in, property was secured, and a copy of the warrant was left at the residence.

A backhoe owned by Lyon County was driven to Tracy from Amiret for the search but was forced out of commission by a leaking hose to the hydraulic system shortly after the excavation started. According to the county sheriff, costs of the excavation would be paid by the county.

Excavating Larson property
(photo from *Tracy Area Headlight Herald*, December 18, 1980)

VICTIMS OF FOUL PLAY

Records from the Tracy Hospital, seized by a prior search warrant, showed that Jean Larson had blood type O. Analyst Laber tested the blood from several areas of the kitchen and it was found to be human type O blood, and all of the blood was of the same enzyme grouping.

In December 1980, Clarence Larson provided a sample of his blood, which was tested by Laber and found to be blood type O. However, Laber's enzyme grouping tests showed that Clarence Larson's blood was not consistent with the enzyme groupings of the above-noted blood stains and spatterings.

Laber said the blood spattering was consistent with a violent blow or blows to a portion of the human body and inconsistent with a cut hand or similar injury. Tests indicated that the blood was no more than two months old, and consistent with that of Jean Larson's blood type.

In reviewing the basement area, the south wall had an area of what appeared to be fresh cement covering approximately 4 foot long by 3 ½ foot wide area. The texture was different from other wall portions in the basement, and it appeared to be very clean. There had been a 1 ½" galvanized steel pipe liner dug into the bottom portion of the south wall in early October.

Ford Ankrum, who assisted in installing the water line, said that the most reasonable way to put in such a device would simply be to drive it through the wall, and there would be absolutely no reason to have a hole anywhere near as large as 4 feet by 3 1/2 feet that had to be covered with new cement. In addition, on the southwest, 15 feet to 20 feet from the west side of the house was a cistern, which could also contain a body.

LARSON CONTACTS
AN ATTORNEY

On December 30, Agents Berg and O'Gorman and Chief Thompson traveled to Arlington, Texas to contact Clarence Larson. New facts and evidence had come to the attention of the above officers since contact was last made with Larson on November 25, 1980, and it was decided that Larson should be contacted and re-interviewed. It was determined that Larson left Omaha, on or about December 29 or 30, with his daughter, Janet, traveling to Arlington, Texas, and Larson would be in Arlington for the next 30 to 60 days.

On December 31, contact was made with Detective Carl Privitt of the Arlington Police Department. The detective was briefed on the purpose of the visit and the facts surrounding the investigation to date.

During the background investigation of Janet Larson, it was revealed that Janet had been recently divorced from

Calvin Bard. Privitt telephoned Janet's residence and a female answered, identifying herself as Mrs. Bard, mother of Calvin Bard. She said that Clarence, Janet, and grandson Steven (or Stephen) Larson left Arlington and were on their way to McAllen, Texas, but she did not know when they would return. Privitt was advised that the three of them left just ten minutes prior to their call. Privitt felt that Mrs. Bard was somewhat confused as to their whereabouts and when they would return. A message was left with Mrs. Bard that when Larson returned, he was to call the Arlington Police Department.

Later that day, Agent Berg made personal contact with Mrs. Bard. She was about seventy-five or eighty years old, senile, and very confused as to the whereabouts of Clarence and Janet. Mrs. Bard provided Berg with her son Calvin's address and phone number so he could be interviewed. The officers checked Calvin's apartment but found no one at home. Then they checked his place of employment and found the office was closed.

On January 1, 1981, Agent Berg went to the apartment and found Calvin at home that morning. Calvin requested to be interviewed at his place of employment, so they met there at 10:15 a.m. During the interview, Calvin said that since they had first contacted him, he made telephone calls to his mother in Arlington, Ron Larson in Omaha, and Mrs. Rita Sterrett in Luverne, Minnesota, attempting to find Clarence's whereabouts. Calvin found out that they were in southern Texas on vacation and weren't sure when they would return. He said that his mother resided at Janet's residence, and was very senile and easily confused as to what was actually going on. Calvin said that he and Janet had been divorced for three or four months, but they owned a business together and had contact daily. Janet told him that her stepmother had gone missing in early October 1980.

Calvin said this did not arouse any suspicion on his part, as the contact he had with Clarence and Jean over the years gave him the impression that the marriage was deteriorating. In a conversation he had with Jean a few years previously, she mentioned that she would like to move to northern Minnesota. Jean was a heavy drinker, but the problem had improved over the last year or so. Calvin had the impression that Jean had no time for Clarence, but Clarence was very concerned about and tolerant of Jean. Calvin said if he heard from Clarence or Janet, he would contact the officers.

Sheriff Van Den Broeke received a telephone call from Larson on January 2, advising that he and his daughter and grandson were in Corpus Christi, Texas and that Clarence had received a call advising him that officers were in Arlington, Texas looking for him. Larson said that they were traveling to McAllen, Texas and they would be returning to Arlington on Sunday, January 4, and left the impression with Van Den Broeke that he would talk to them when he returned.

On January 3, an Arlington Police car drove by the residence and noticed Janet's car parked in the driveway at approximately 5 p.m. Agent Berg called the residence and the phone was answered by Steven Larson. He advised that Clarence and his mother left a few minutes ago to make a call to an undisclosed party. Steven said they should return within the hour. Contact was finally made by telephone at 9:30 p.m. Janet advised that her father was sleeping and stated that Clarence had planned to fly to Sioux Falls, South Dakota on January 4, and there contact an attorney by the name of Trygstad. Janet said that her father's attorney told him not to talk to any law enforcement officers prior to talking to Trygstad.

Janet contacted Agent Berg at the Arlington Police Department on the morning of January 4. She stated that her father left the airport at 8:30 that morning for Sioux Falls and agreed to meet with Agents Berg and O'Gorman and Chief Deputy Thompson for an interview.

During the interview, she stated that she and her son, Steven, had gone to Omaha for the Christmas holidays and that on December 30, 1980, she, along with her son and father, traveled from Omaha to Arlington. They then left Arlington on December 31 for a short vacation to southern Texas, including Corpus Christi and McAllen, Texas; returning to Arlington on January 3 in the late afternoon. She said that while they were in Corpus Christi, her father received a phone call from Ronald Larson, advising Clarence that officers from Minnesota were in Texas wishing to speak to him. Janet did not know the substance of the conversation, as she stepped out of the room when the phone call was placed.

Upon returning to Arlington on January 3, Janet observed an unmarked police vehicle sitting outside her residence and was advised by her mother-in-law that several officers had been at the residence inquiring about Clarence. It was then that Clarence decided to contact an attorney by the name of Trygstad in Sioux Falls for advice. Janet said that because they felt her phone might be bugged, they left the residence and used a public phone to contact the attorney. Upon contacting Trygstad, Larson was advised to fly to Sioux Falls on January 4 to meet with the attorney at noon. Clarence was not to make contact with any law enforcement officers prior to meeting with him (Trygstad). Janet said that other than the initial story her father told her in October 1980, she had no other knowledge and did not discuss the matter with her father during this time.

Upon returning to Minnesota, Agent Berg had a conversation with Van Den Broeke, who advised that his office received a telephone call from David Trygstad on January 2, at approximately 11:52. The substance of that call was that Trygstad had been retained by Larson and that Trygstad called to determine why Minnesota officers were in Texas talking to his client and requested to know whether there were any outstanding warrants for Larson. Trygstad was advised that there were no outstanding warrants and that the Minnesota officers were in Texas only to talk to his client.

It should be pointed out that in the conversation with Janet, she indicated that her father had first contacted the attorney on January 4. However, this phone call seems to indicate that the attorney was contacted prior to that date. It was also learned that Trygstad had made several attempts to contact Agent Berg and Agent O'Gorman, leaving messages at the Worthington office and the Mankato office, as well as at the Lyon County Sheriff's Department. Trygstad was to be contacted later.

On January 6, two attorneys from Sioux Falls, representing Clarence Larson, showed up at the Larson home and contacted local police. They examined the house and then left. There was nothing more reported about Trygstad in the file.

BLOODY PILLOWCASE
FOUND

AGENT BERG WAS contacted by Chief Deputy Thompson on January 10, 1981, explaining he had information from Highway Patrol Officer Bernard Hill of Marshall, that a dog owned by Fabian Maher of Currie had carried home a bloody pillowcase. The Mahers live in Murray County near the Shetek State Park, which is approximately 10 miles south of Tracy, and that the pillowcase might be connected with the missing person investigation.

Thompson advised Berg about a hired man, employed by Clarence Larson about nineteen or twenty years ago, who was found hanging by the neck from a tree located within the boundaries of Shetek State Park. Rumor was that Clarence Larson was suspected as having been involved somehow in his death. According to rumor, Clarence Larson and the unnamed hired man had a disagreement about back wages owed him in the amount of $1400 or $1500, and about a week or two after the disagreement, the hired man was found hanging from a tree in Shetek State Park. Any involvement in the incident by Clarence Larson was purely speculative at the time.

Agent Berg, Murray County Sheriff Jack Lewis, and Conservation Officer Floyd Ragen contacted Mr. and Mrs. Fabian Maher at their home in Currie on January 12, 1981 and learned that Mrs. Maher discovered a fairly new pillowcase, soaked with blood, lying on their front yard sometime in October 1980. At the time, she thought one of her dogs carried the pillowcase home, and initially thought one of her children had used the pillowcase for hunting or trapping. The pillowcase was new, white in color with no designs on it, and soaked with a large quantity of blood. She said the blood stains were not consistent with someone having used it to wipe up blood or to wipe blood off their hands. After she inspected the pillowcase, it was thrown into a trash barrel and burnt with other rubbish, with nothing left of it. Mrs. Maher checked with her neighbors to identify the source of the pillowcase and none of them knew where it came from either.

Mrs. Maher said that their dog was a large German Shepherd, a spayed female and the dog did not roam for any great distances; not more than a two-mile radius of the residence.

Mrs. Maher said that she was familiar with the background of Clarence Larson but did not know him personally. She talked about the hired man found hanging from a tree in the area known as the Hanover Farm, which was approximately one mile northeast of their farmhouse.

AERIAL SEARCH

ON JANUARY 14, a state helicopter searched near Lake Shetek and Shetek State Park, in an area approximately two miles in radius around the Maher farm. During the course of the search, nothing of interest was discovered. The search was conducted by the State BCA and officers from several other agencies. Following the search of the area around the Maher farm, a search of the old Clarence Larson farm located in Murray County, Lake Sarah Township was also conducted, but nothing of interest was found there either.

A PSYCHIC IS HIRED

By THE END of January 1981, there were no new leads and an overall review of the case was conducted at the county attorney's office in Marshall. Taking part were the Tracy police, the Lyon County sheriff's office, the county attorney's office, and the BCA team. A suggestion was made by Chief Healy that the involvement of a psychic should be considered. After a lengthy discussion with all investigators involved in the case, it was decided that Mr. Maurice Dykshoorn, a clairvoyant from New York City, should be contacted to determine his availability and what the cost would be.

Dykshoorn was contacted and agreed to assist in the investigation. He was scheduled to come to Minnesota on April 20, 1981. There was no fee for his services, but the requesting agency would have to bear the cost of travel expenses for Dykshoorn and his wife. Dykshoorn was originally from Holland, then moved to Australia in 1960. In 1970 he moved to the United States, where he assisted law enforcement in one hundred homicide cases with much success in helping clear those cases.

Psychic Dykshoorn (in white coat) at Larson home
(photo from *Tracy Area Headlight Herald*, April 23, 1981)

On April 20, 1981, Agents Berg and O'Gorman picked up Dykshoorn and his wife at the airport in Minneapolis and traveled to Marshall, where they checked into a hotel in the area. Deputy Thompson and the Lyon County Attorney prepared a search warrant to allow access to the Larson residence on April 21 for the purpose of having Dykshoorn inspect the premises and to take additional measurements of the blood spatterings in the kitchen area, and to search for any and all blunt instruments. The only information given to Dykshoorn at the time was that it was a missing persons investigation involving Leona Jean Larson and that she had been missing for six months. Dykshoorn told the officers that he did not want any further information regarding the case. By using his psychic powers, he would determine what transpired on the date in question, and after he was done, he would advise the officers what he felt had happened and allow questions at that time.

On the morning of April 21, Agents Berg and O'Gorman, Chief Healy, Sheriff Van Den Broeke, Deputy Thompson, and Dykshoorn arrived at the Larson residence. Almost immediately upon entering the kitchen area of the residence, Dykshoorn began to make a gasping and gagging sound. He grabbed his neck area with both hands and began to fall backwards toward the kitchen sink. He made the statement, "She is dead, you know. It happened here," referring to the kitchen area.

Dykshoorn said he sees an older, sickly type woman, 5'3," 110 pounds, being strangled by an older man, about 60 years old, 5'10" to 5'11," and heavy-set. He demonstrated the way the older man walked, in an upright position with shoulders back and toes pointed outward. This was indeed the way Larson walked. Dykshoorn saw an argument between the man and woman. The argument was over the sale of some property, possibly the house itself. He felt the man wanted to move to a warmer climate, and the woman did not want to leave. During the argument, the man grabbed the woman by the throat; she passed out and fell to the floor directly in front of the kitchen sink. The man went out into the garage

VICTIMS OF FOUL PLAY

area and returned with a blunt instrument, possibly a crowbar, and struck the woman several times on the back of the head. Dykshoorn felt the man shot the woman in the back of the head with a five-shot revolver, possibly a .32-caliber. Dykshoorn said the man owned two pistols and also several long guns.

Dykshoorn said that a section of the carpet in the kitchen had been replaced to conceal bloodstains in the original carpet. (It should be pointed out that a section of carpet in front of the sink had been replaced. However, at the time Dykshoorn made this observation, this section was covered by a throw rug and was not visible to him).

He said that after the killing, the body was wrapped in a tarp, or sheet of heavy plastic, possibly green in color, and that the body and tarp were then wrapped with a nylon-type cord, blue and white in color. Later, he pointed out to those present a crowbar and a piece of blue and white cord hanging on the north wall of the kitchen and advised that the crowbar was the blunt instrument and the section of cord was very similar to that used to wrap around the body and tarp. Both items were then seized as evidence. Chemical testing on the bar strongly indicated the presence of blood on the curved end of the bar, but insufficient amounts were detected for further testing.

He said that because the older man was somewhat crippled, due to arthritis or a bad back, he solicited the assistance of another male to remove the body from the house. He said the body was removed within 48 hours and the younger man loaded the body into the back of an old, beat-up station wagon and that the two men drove the body out of Tracy. By using his psychic powers, he would be able to pinpoint the location where the body was placed, and later give a description and more clues with which to identify the second individual.

The officers, at Dykshoorn's direction, drove east on Highway 14 out of Tracy toward Walnut Grove, then turned south into Walnut Grove. There, we circled around the block and through an alley, eventually returning to Highway 14 and continuing eastbound. He said this was the route taken by the two men. He was not able to explain why they had taken the detour—possibly to determine if they were being followed or not. The younger man was driving and the older man was sitting in the right front seat. He felt the two men knew where they were going but did not know where the body would eventually end up.

From Walnut Grove, the investigators continued eastbound on 14 to Redwood County Road 10 and north on this road to the Cottonwood River located approximately four miles north of Highway 14, where they were instructed to stop by Dykshoorn. He said the two men stopped on the south side of the bridge going over the Cottonwood River, then exited the vehicle.

The younger man carried the body, still wrapped in the tarp, east along the south side of the river. He said the older man walked with the younger man for a distance of approximately 100 yards, and then returned to the vehicle. The young man continued with the body for a distance of about 300 yards east of County Road 10, where he turned into a wooded area located along the river. The young man unwrapped the body and weighted it with some rocks and placed it in the river. Dykshoorn stated that he felt the body was still in the river and that it would be found in this area

VICTIMS OF FOUL PLAY

or a short distance downstream.

After marking the area, the investigators returned to the vehicle, then returned to Highway 14 and into Walnut Grove. Dykshoorn felt that the two men stopped at Anderson's Trucking in Walnut Grove, where the young man got out of the vehicle, walked around the building, and talked to two possible employees of Anderson Trucking. Dykshoorn said the two men knew this younger male and he may have worked for them at one time as a truck driver.

Then the young man got into the station wagon. They drove across the street, stopping at Revere County Co-op Fertilizer Plant, where the young man exited the vehicle and spoke with four men, one of which was a tall man, whom he knew by name. The young man got back into the station wagon and drove to Tracy, where they stopped at the State Highway Department shop, just one block east of the Larson residence on Highway 14. The young man got out of the vehicle and got into another vehicle, which was parked in the lot. The older man drove the station wagon west on Highway 14 to the driveway on Craig Avenue and there turned into the driveway.

The investigators then went back to the State Highway Department shop and Dykshoorn, using his psychic powers, followed the vehicle. They continued westbound on Highway 14 to Highway 59, and north on 59 to the city of Marshall.

Once in Marshall, they went to the 400 block of North 6th Street in Marshall, where Dykshoorn pointed out three houses. The houses were 404, 406, and 407 North 6th Street. Dykshoorn said the younger man either resided in one of these houses and/or is well known by the people who lived in the three above mentioned houses. Dykshoorn said the vehicle driven by the young man was a gray-colored compact car, possibly a Mazda or similar type.

The investigators then returned to Tracy and questioned Dykshoorn. He provided the following information. He stated that he felt the time of death would have been on a Sunday, and the body would have been removed from the residence within 48 hours of death. He stated that the younger man who assisted in removing the body from the residence was not involved in the actual death; that he was only doing a favor for Mr. Larson in assisting him in getting rid of the body. He said that the younger man was about thirty years of age, 5'9" to 5'10," 170 pounds, a muscular-type build, possibly lifted weights in the past; he might have trouble with his left knee, might have been a truck driver, possibly for Anderson Trucking. He stated that he saw this younger man as having received some money from Mr. Larson, as a result of helping remove the body or possibly having worked with Mr. Larson in the past. He further advised that this younger man might be bisexual, and that there might be some connection between himself and Mr. Larson's son, Ronald Larson.

Dykshoorn described Mrs. Larson as a sickly-type woman; she favored her right side, possibly as a result of a knee or hip injury. He believed she had trouble with her pancreas, she might have had an enlarged liver, and she might have some type of blood disorder. She might also have broken or cracked ribs as a result of beatings sustained from her husband.

He described Mr. Larson as heavy-set, with back or leg ailments. He believed Mr. Larson was a very mean-type individual, that he may possibly be a sexual sadist, and that he perceives himself as somewhat of a ladies' man, and that he was sexually very active for his age.

Dykshoorn felt that Mr. Larson told his son about killing Mrs. Larson; however, he did not feel that Ron knew the details of the incident, nor did he believe that Ron knew where the body was located or that he had anything to do with the actual death. He said that he felt Clarence had told several people that his wife had a considerable amount of money; however, he did not feel this was true. He felt that Clarence received approximately $3,000 from the sale of his wife's personal effects. He stated that he felt that Clarence Larson removed some money and/or jewelry from a safety-deposit box. He felt that Mr. Larson had two separate banking accounts, one under his own name and one under an assumed name, possibly at the First Northwestern Bank in Marshall.

Dykshoorn indicated that a younger male individual had assisted in removing the body of Jean Larson from the residence in October 1980. He felt the younger male had either lived at or had been associated at one of three homes located on North 6th Street in Marshall, and that the male drove a gray compact car.

On May 6, 1981, agents interviewed three individuals living on North 6th Street. One of the homes was that of Mrs. Zerfas. She said that she did not know Clarence Larson, nor did any of her children have any connection with Mr. Larson or anyone else from the Tracy area.

A second interview was conducted at the Lyon County Sheriff's office. During that interview, Mr. Thomas Sullivan said that he was not familiar with Clarence Larson or anyone else from Tracy, and none of his children were acquainted with Larson either.

During the third interview, Mr. Richard Marron stated that he had no connection with Clarence Larson; he did know several people in Tracy but had no connection with Clarence Larson.

These three individuals were shown the composite compiled by Dykshoorn and advised that they knew no one who resembled the composite or drove a gray compact car allegedly driven by a young male. It appeared there was no connection between these three families and the Jean Larson investigation—another dead end.

Officers conducted a search of the Cottonwood River at its intersection with County Road 10 on April 27, 1981. The search was conducted from the bridge crossing the Cottonwood River for approximately one-half mile downstream; nothing of interest was found.

On May 15, 1981, Sgt. Ray K. Johnson, Criminal Investigations Division, Alexandria Police Department, wrote a letter to Chief Thomas Healy which said, "On May 14, 1981, Mr. Marinus Dykshoorn stopped in at our Department and used our photo fit kit to make a composite for you in reference to your case (Leona Jean Larson). He requested that I send you a copy. Hope this helps."

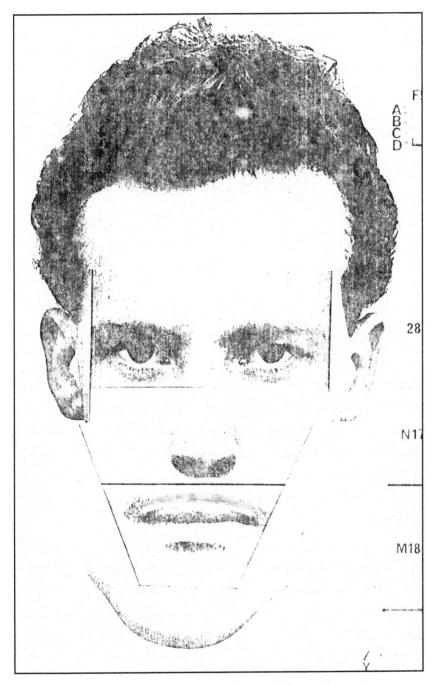

**Composite photo of young male
from investigation file, Tracy Police Department**

INVESTIGATION
CONTINUES

AGENT BERG RECEIVED information from Deputy Ronald McClure of the Rock County Sheriff's office indicating that during the first two or three weeks in May 1981, he had observed a 1971 Chevrolet parked in front of the Sterrett residence in Luverne, Minnesota. Agent Berg and Deputy McClure interviewed Rita Sterrett at her residence on May 26, 1981.

<u>Rita Sterrett</u> had previously been interviewed on December 17, 1980 and had indicated at that time that she attended beauty school in Sioux Falls, South Dakota with Janet Larson, and that because of this acquaintance, she had become friendly with Clarence and Jean Larson over the last several years. She stated that on October 31, 1980, she received a telephone call from Clarence Larson advising her

that he was traveling to Omaha to visit his son and asked if he could stop and visit on his way through. He arrived at her residence and spent the evening with her prior to leaving for Omaha. Clarence told her that Jean was in California and after the holidays he was going to fly to California from Omaha to meet her. He did not say why she was there. The last time she saw Jean was in January 1980, when she was in Tracy for a visit.

During the May 26 interview, Sterrett said that Larson had been living at the Sterrett residence for about three weeks prior to his returning to Tracy in May 1981. Rita said that there was very little talk about Jean's disappearance, and she could not remember any specifics. However, she did remember that at one point, Clarence mentioned that his wife's drinking had cost him a considerable amount of money over the years.

Sterrett was asked if she was curious about Jean's disappearance and responded that during a conversation she had with Janet Larson during Christmas time (1980), she had asked Janet what was going on. Janet told Sterrett, "We've talked about that, and we've decided that it's best for you that you don't know anything about it." Since that time, Sterrett had accepted this and had not made any inquiries about the incident.

Sterrett also stated it was her opinion that Clarence was concerned about the investigation being conducted, but she did not feel Clarence was concerned about his wife being gone.

Agent Berg asked Sterrett if she would be willing to pass along any and all information, which she might obtain from Larson relative to his wife's disappearance, on to law enforcement authorities. She said she would have to think about it before making a decision. She said she would contact Berg during the week of June 1, 1981. It should be pointed out that Berg did not tell Sterrett any specific questions to ask, nor was she coached as to how to obtain any information from Larson. No new evidence ever came forth from Sterrett, that we know of.

At the request of David Peterson, Assistant Lyon County Attorney, Ronald Larson was interviewed in Omaha on June 3, 1981, to determine whether he and his father, Clarence, had any conversations regarding Jean's disappearance.
At about 6:00 p.m., Agents Berg and O'Gorman interviewed Ron in Room 485 of the New Tower Inn Motel in Omaha. The following information was obtained.

Ronald Larson indicated that he and his father had very little conversation regarding his stepmother's disappearance. He said he first became aware Jean was missing sometime in October 1980 when he traveled to Tracy to visit his father. The initial story his father told him was that Jean had gone to the Twin Cities and from there had traveled to Wisconsin. However, Ron indicated to his father that he did not believe him and was then informed by Clarence that Jean left sometime around 2 a.m., had yelled upstairs that she was leaving him, and gotten into a car and left. This contradicted the story Clarence gave during his interview on November 25, 1980, when Larson indicated he had not heard or seen a vehicle leaving the area on the night of his wife's disappearance.

Ron was questioned as to whether his father or stepmother planned on moving from Tracy to a warmer climate for the winter months. He indicated that his father never discussed this with him and there was no intention of going south for the winter that he was aware of.

Ron was asked if he had any idea why his father had contacted two attorneys in Sioux Falls, South Dakota shortly after the investigators' attempted contact with him in Arlington, Texas. Ron stated he received a call from his father in December 1980, advising that agents were in Texas attempting to contact him. Upon learning this, Ron told his father to "get his butt out of there" and to contact an attorney. Ron advised he told his father this because Ron had been railroaded by law enforcement on several occasions, and he did not want to see his father railroaded in this matter. Ron gave his father a quantity of money with which to retain the two attorneys out of Sioux Falls, and said that he did not expect to receive the money back. When Ron was asked if he had any idea what happened to Jean, he stated, "I don't know, and like I told her daughter, I don't care." When asked if he would care if she were dead, he stated, "Not really. I could care less." Ron saw his stepmother as an alcoholic who drank excessively, and whenever he was present, there were no arguments or physical abuse by either one of them that he was aware of.

Ron was asked about the relationship between his father and Rita Sterrett. He said that Rita was a friend of his father and stepmother, and they had met Rita through his sister, Janet. Ron was asked if he knew his father had stayed with Mrs. Sterrett after returning to Minnesota in May of 1981, and Ron stated that he had not known that, but it was none of his business anyway.

Ron was asked what type of weapons his father would have access to in October 1980. Ron said there were two or three .22-caliber revolvers at the Larson residence in Tracy and they were owned by Ron. While he was in Tracy for the auction on October 26, 1980, Ron picked up these guns and brought them back to Omaha with him. He still retained possession of them.

It should be noted that upon initial contact with Ron on June 3, while attempting to set up this interview, he refused to meet with the agents, advising that he also had retained an attorney in this matter and that he would not talk to them. However, after a brief discussion, Ron consented to the interview and agreed to meet at the New Tower Inn in Omaha. Because of this initial hostility toward Agents Berg and O'Gorman, they were somewhat uncertain as to the cooperation which they would receive from Mr. Larson concerning the investigation. Due to this uncertainty, it was decided that the interview would be recorded without Mr. Larson's knowledge.

REWARD OFFERED

ON JULY 2, 1981 it was reported in the *Tracy Area Headlight Herald* that the investigation was still in progress and that a $1,000 reward was offered for information concerning the whereabouts of Leona Jean Larson. All information would be treated confidentially, and any assistance in the matter would be appreciated. After this date, it seems the investigation went cold and nothing more was reported in the local newspapers. Jean's body has never been recovered. It remains an open, missing persons case to this day.

REPORT ON PHYSICAL EVIDENCE

AGENT BERG RECEIVED a report from the BCA crime lab on July 23, 1981. The following evidence was received by the laboratory on December 2-3, 1980:

> Item 35: One knife rack containing six knives removed from kitchen wall above sink.
>
> Item 37: One manila envelope containing hair from middle left sink door.
>
> Item 38: One manila envelope containing hair from south wall of kitchen.
>
> Item 39: One manila envelope containing hair from mop board of south kitchen wall.
>
> Item 40: One envelope containing curlers.

The following additional evidence was received in the laboratory by Terry Laber on June 3, 1981 by US mail.

Item 45: One manila envelope said to contain hair from Clarence Larson.

Here are the results of the examinations.

One (1) questioned hair from the knife rack (Item 35), three (3) from the south wall in kitchen (Item 38), and three (3) from the south wall mop board in kitchen (Item 39) were consistent as having come from the same source as the hairs found on the curlers (Item 40).

One (1) questioned hair from left sink door in kitchen (Item 37) and one (1) from the south wall mop board in kitchen (Item 39) were (gray) colorless hairs that could have come from either source, curlers (Item 40) or from Clarence Larson (Item 45).

The other questioned hairs, five (5) from left sink door in kitchen (Item 37) and three (3) from south wall in kitchen (Item 38) were found to be non-human hairs.

The report was certified by Mary Ann Strauss, Crime Laboratory Analyst.

On November 19, 1982, Agent Berg conducted a driver's license computer check of the 48 Continental United States under the name of Leona Jean Larson. The results were a valid Minnesota driver's license with no violations. The license was set to expire on October 13, 1984. The other states queried indicated that there were no other driver's licenses on file under that name and date of birth.

≈◇≈

On November 23, 1982, Agent Berg contacted Bob Spanger, Administrative Supervisor for the Social Security Administration in Marshall, Minnesota requesting verification as to whether Leona Jean Larson's Social Security check was still being held in escrow. Spanger indicated there was no change in the status of Leona Jean Larson's account. He advised that the Social Security payments were retained in escrow and that they were periodically reviewed. He advised that Mrs. Larson's account would remain as is until there was some significant change in her status. Spanger indicated that if there would be a change in this account, he would contact Berg at the Worthington office.

On October 27, 1995, BCA Special Agent Paul Soppeland spoke with Terry Cinkle, Social Security Administrative Claims Representative in Marshall. Cinkle confirmed that Jean Larson had been declared dead in November 1994, she had not been receiving any Social Security benefits since the checks were stopped in March 1981 until November of 1994, and there had been no contact with Mrs. Larson during that time, and no one received any of her checks. Soppeland asked Cinkle if anyone would be entitled to her checks. Cinkle stated that any widower in a case like this, once the wife had been declared dead, would be entitled to widower's benefits. Cinkle said, when their office was notified of the Declaration of Death, that Social Security initiated the widower's benefits to Clarence Larson. Cinkle said he could not reveal the amount of any benefits that Larson was receiving, nor could he tell the location where they were being sent without a signed authorization from Clarence Larson.

In June 1983, agent Berg received a telephone call from Chief of Police Kurt Wiese of the Tracy Police Department indicating that he had conversations with two deputies of the Murray County Sheriff's office. They indicated that during dragging operations for a drowning victim on Lake Shetek in Murray County, they hooked an object which they believed to be the body of the drowning victim. Upon removing the item from the water, they discovered it was not the drowning victim but rather a partial sheet of clear plastic with a five pound window sash attached to it. They felt it may have some connections with the disappearance of Jean Larson because Clarence Larson would have been familiar with this area. A decision was made to conduct a limited under water search of the area where the plastic and window sash were discovered.

On August 24, 1984, officers met at Lake Shetek and conducted an under water search of a limited portion of that lake. After five hours of searching, the search was called off. The only thing found was a canine skull. Due to the murky condition of the water, visibility for the divers was zero, and this hampered any search operation. No further searches were ever conducted in the lake.

INVESTIGATION UPDATE

AN INVESTIGATION UPDATE on April 7, 1983: Agent Berg, BCA, and Curt Weise, Tracy Police Chief re-interviewed the following individuals: Mary DeBlieck, Cora Peterson, Roy Deal, Diane Deming, William Koch, Kathy Hohler, and Duane Wiese to determine whether any

Leona Jean Larson
Photo from NamUs.gov

additional information had come to their attention. They all stated they had no additional information which could benefit this investigation. They had no contact with Jean nor knew her current whereabouts. They had seen Clarence from time to time, but never discussed the disappearance of his wife. They stated that Clarence stayed by himself most of the time and had little contact with the people of Tracy.

AMENDMENT TO
MINNESOTA LAW

BEFORE **1981,** IT was nearly impossible to charge a suspect with murder without the body as evidence. An amendment to a Minnesota law in 1981 changed that, but only if the fact of death can be proven with circumstantial evidence beyond a reasonable doubt. But because Leona Jean Larson's disappearance occurred before the 1981 amendment, her body had become a necessity for murder charges to be filed. Clarence Larson has since passed away on March 18, 2002 at the age of 91. He is buried next to Martha and his granddaughter Debra Jean in the Zion Lutheran Church Cemetery near Balaton.

RUMORS AND HEARSAY

I PREPARED A list of some of the many stories that people still talk about to this day whenever anyone mentions the name Clarence Larson. Please be advised that this list of rumors and hearsay cannot be confirmed or denied, and I am hereby held harmless for reporting them here.

After Martha's death and Jean's disappearance, many stories circulated around the Tracy area about Clarence and the suspicious activities he may have been involved with. He continued his life in Tracy as though nothing bad had ever happened to his two wives. He obtained some nefarious nicknames such as "Killer Larson" and "PTO Larson," and other names that won't be repeated here. Anytime the people of Tracy set their eyes upon Clarence, they tended to walk the other way. People felt he got away with murdering Martha and probably Jean too. Although Jean's body has never been found, Clarence was suspected of murdering her and disposing of her body somewhere. Most people suspected that Jean's remains were in the Lyon County landfill, and there were many other theories about where she might be buried.

There are so many stories about Clarence from Tracy residents that I had to try to find out what was fact and what was fiction. I spent numerous hours reviewing old issues of newspapers on microfilm from the *Tracy Area Headlight Herald*, *Murray County Herald*, *Cottonwood County Citizen*, and the *Windom Reporter*, so I could try to determine what was a true story and what was just rumor or hearsay. Below are some stories reported in newspapers, but nothing confirmed that Clarence was the suspect in any of them. I'm sure there are many more stories out there that I've never even heard about yet.

One of the rumors I heard was that Clarence murdered his hired hand, Gerald (Gilly) Pearsoll because he had a life insurance policy out on him, but this could not be substantiated. This rumor could have started because Freeman Pearsoll was Gerald's brother and it was reported that Freeman committed suicide. I spoke with several people in the Tracy area about this, but no one could remember the date this took place. Below are newspaper articles which might have sparked the rumors that Clarence murdered his hired hand. Of course, if the hired man they were referring to was Gilly, this was not true, because Gerald (Gilly) Pearsoll died June 29, 1981.

November 16, 1950, Tracy Area Headlight-Herald

"2 Commit Suicide Within Three Days – Two bachelors, living within a few miles of Tracy, took their own lives within a period of three days. Dr. H.D. Patterson, Murray county coroner, stated that Freeman Pearsoll, a man in his 50s, took his life when he strangled himself at his home north of Currie on Lake Shetek on Saturday, November 11.

"Karl Swenson, a Walnut Grove odd job laborer in his 40s, took his life on Monday night, November 13, when he shot himself in the head with a shotgun in his garage."

November 16, 1950, Murray County Herald

"Currie Farmer Takes Own Life – Freeman Pearsoll, 56-year-old, Currie farm hand was found dead Saturday noon, his body hanging from a tree limb near his farm home. The verdict reached by County Coroner Dr. Hugh Patterson and Sheriff George Nelson was that he had taken his own life. In recent years, Pearsoll had worked on farms near Currie. He was last employed by Lloyd Grinde, a farmer south of Currie, but was preparing a farm he had rented near the Fritz home and Kosak farm when his death occurred.

"Pearsoll's body was found, frozen, by John Kosak Jr., at noon on Saturday. Joe Hollis, also of Currie, was with Kosak when he found the corpse kneeling beneath a tree with the rope tight around his neck. The body was found about 70 yards north of the farm home, owned by a Mrs. August Pearson of Balaton and formerly known as the old Hanover place.

"The doors to Pearsoll's home were locked and his personal belongings were in it. He was apparently moved in and about prepared for winter. According to neighbors he had recently purchased a used tractor to be employed in farm work next spring. He had also purchased a supply of groceries at Currie a few days before his death.

"Broken twigs and other marks in the tree, indicate that Pearsoll had climbed on the branch (about six feet high) and dropped from there with the noose around his neck.

"There was considerable speculation by the coroner before he arrived at the suicide verdict. No one could reach an explanation of his actions, in view of the fact that he had obviously planned far in advance for his farm work. However, his personal jewelry and wallet were found unmolested in the house, and no other motive for murder was suggested. An examination of the body in Slayton revealed no other marks and the cause of death was reported as strangulation by Dr. Patterson."

Another story was that one day, as Martha Larson was driving to Balaton, she had trouble with her car. As she was driving down the road, the car started to make a weird noise and was hard to control. She finally pulled over on the shoulder, shut off the engine, exited the vehicle, and checked the tires. She noticed that the lug nuts were loose. She did not know how this could happen, but it appeared that someone may have loosened the lug nuts, which could have caused her to lose control of the vehicle and have a terrible accident. This incident was not reported in the newspapers.

Another rumor was that Clarence was said to have been involved in a hunting accident up north somewhere near Hibbing. The story goes that Clarence accidentally shot Oliver Sande, so that Clarence could have Jean all to himself. It was well-known that Clarence spent time at the Sande residence during deer-hunting season, but it appears this accidental shooting was just a rumor, because Oliver Sande died in 1999, and Walter Kronman, Jean's first husband, died of a heart attack in April 1978.

Clarence and his father, Carl, reportedly owned a small cabin up north somewhere. There was a story that one day the cabin mysteriously caught on fire. Someone saw the smoke and notified the fire department. The fire crew arrived at the scene and put out the fire, but later that day, somehow smoldering embers started up the fire again and the cabin burned to the ground. Clarence claimed that he was not there when the cabin burned, but it was rumored he collected an undetermined amount of money from the insurance company.

Then there was a story about a small barn on Clarence's farm which caught fire and burned to the ground in 1945. It wasn't much of a barn; the center of it was built to a first-floor level, there was no roof, and there was a lean-to on each side of the main section. One day, Clarence had the tractor hooked up to the manure spreader and parked the spreader in front of the barn door. Clarence claimed the tractor backfired and set the hay on fire. He collected an unknown sum of money from the insurance company. This fire was not reported in the newspapers, but a neighbor told me this fire did happen sometime in 1945.

Then there was the second barn fire in June 1955, which I have previously reported in the story. It started around midnight on a clear, moonlit night, and there was no wind.

The barn was a total loss. Clarence reported to the insurance company that he had several hundred bales of hay and many bushels of corn and flax in the barn. Again, Clarence collected an unknown sum of money from the insurance company.

Sometime in the 1970s, Clarence was hired to paint the interior of the Tracy Bakery. One day, while he was on a ladder painting the ceiling, he lost his balance, grabbed the ceiling fan, and cut his fingers. It was said that one finger or part of a finger was cut off. He was taken to the Tracy Hospital for medical treatment. His hand was stitched and wrapped up. He was held overnight for observation. I did not find anything reported in the newspapers that confirmed this story; however, a retired nurse whom I interviewed confirmed that she was working that day and saw his hand all wrapped up. There were rumors that Clarence staged the accident so he could collect insurance money from the owner of the bakery. There were no other details regarding this story.

Another story I heard was that Clarence tried to electrocute his stepdaughter, Olivia. It seems Olivia and Clarence never did get along. It was rumored that Clarence somehow rigged up electrical wires around the base of the basement shower. Jean normally never used the basement shower, but Olivia sometimes did. Olivia might have seen the wires, became suspicious, and never used that shower again. A subsequent owner of the house did find evidence of odd electrical wiring around the base of the shower. They removed the shower and the wiring immediately.

Shortly after Jean disappeared, the story goes that Clarence shot Jean's dog in the kitchen and asked a neighbor to come by and bury the dog in the back yard. This story was confirmed by a family member I interviewed. She knew the neighbor who buried the dog for Clarence.

Another rumor was that Clarence was in the back of the Scandia Café early one morning and when he came into the café, a waitress noticed lipstick all over his collar. There were no further details reported regarding this incident.

It was rumored that Clarence may have been stalking a sixteen-year-old girl who worked at the Red Owl grocery store in Tracy. It was said that Clarence would come into the store frequently, purchase a few items, and always end up in the line where the young girl was cashiering. While waiting in the check-out line, he'd manage to strike up a conversation with her. The girl was friendly with all her customers, so talking with Clarence was no different. Eleanor, another woman who worked at the store, happened to notice Clarence being a bit too friendly with the young girl. Before Jean's disappearance, Clarence came into the store one day and asked the girl if she would cashier at his rummage sale. Later that day, the girl mentioned this to Eleanor, and she replied, "Oh no you're not." Eleanor informed the girl of Clarence's past. When the story of Jean's disappearance spread through the town, Eleanor kept a watchful eye on the young girl. If Clarence was in the store, Eleanor would quickly trade places with the girl so she would not have to interact with Clarence. The girl would wait in the back of the store until he left. After Jean

VICTIMS OF FOUL PLAY

disappeared, a young man who worked at the store as the meat cutter offered to follow the young girl home every night to make sure she got home safely.

There was the story of a young woman on a bike who was riding through Tracy sometime after Jean's disappearance. Clarence happened to see her in the grocery store. She appeared to have been on a long journey and looked like she could use a shower and a home-cooked meal, so Clarence invited her to his house where she could clean up and have a nice meal. The woman accepted the invitation, not knowing anything about Clarence's past, and followed him home. A woman who was at the grocery store that day heard about Clarence's encounter with the young woman and felt the need to check on the situation. She drove by the Larson residence and saw the two talking outside in the yard at Larson's home. When she arrived home, she called the police, informing them of the incident. They told her they would check on things. Later that evening, the police called the woman, informing her that the young lady was very grateful the police came by to check on her and get her out of the house. There were no further details to this story.

There was the story of a nineteen-year-old Tracy woman who disappeared on April 2, 1987. She was last seen about 1:30 a.m. at a party in Revere, and it was rumored that Clarence happened to be in the vicinity during the time of her disappearance. There was an article in the *Tracy Area Headlight Herald* which was probably the source of the rumor that Clarence was somehow involved. The story of the disappearance of Michelle Klein was reported in the newspaper on April 8, 1987. Michelle's body was discovered a few days after her disappearance, by canoeists in Pell Creek about a mile east of Revere. The cause of death was listed as "possible exposure and fresh-water drowning." Temperatures on the morning of her disappearance dipped below freezing. The sheriff said there was no evidence of foul play in her death.

I recently heard a story that a man delivered a load of fuel oil to the Larson farm site a couple days after Martha's death. He wanted to leave the bill for the delivery and knocked on the door, but there was no response. He peeked in the window and saw what appeared to be some blood spatter on the walls and other areas in the kitchen. This could not be confirmed.

Then there were rumors that a few weeks after Jean's disappearance, someone saw her in a women's shelter in Marshall. Another source claimed they had seen Jean somewhere in South Dakota much later. No one was ever able to confirm these sightings.

It was rumored that one night after Jean disappeared, four young kids, ages eight or nine, made a sign and placed it in the front yard of the Larson residence late at night. It read "Mrs. Larson is dead and gone but Killer Larson lives on and on." The sign was later removed from the property.

These are just a few of the many stories, rumors, and accusations that developed when Clarence Larson, a murder suspect in his first wife's death, was acquitted of murder, and then his second wife disappeared. I'm quite sure there

VICTIMS OF FOUL PLAY

are countless stories that have yet to be heard. Clarence continued living in Tracy for fifteen years after Jean disappeared. What kind of a life did he have? Nobody associated with him. He stayed in his house like a hermit most of the time.

WHAT HAPPENED TO JEAN?

MOST LIKELY IT started with another argument on the night of October 5, 1980. Harsh words between the two escalated, causing Clarence to probably put his large hands around Jean's neck, choking her. In Dykshoorn's report, he saw Jean being choked, passing out, and falling to the floor in front of the kitchen sink. He then saw Clarence go to the garage, get a crowbar and strike Jean in the back of the head several times. Then if that weren't enough, Dykshoorn stated Clarence got a revolver and shot her in the back of the head. According to Dykshoorn with his psychic abilities, this is how Jean's life ended. So now, what to do with the body? Dykshoorn said that Clarence wrapped the body up in a tarp or a sheet of heavy plastic, then tied it up with a nylon cord. Dykshoorn saw the crowbar and cord hanging on a wall in the kitchen. Traces of blood were found on the crowbar, so more than likely, this was the blunt instrument used as the weapon.

Terry Laber, a qualified BCA laboratory chemist experienced in homicide investigations, tested the blood and human flesh discovered in the kitchen, and found it to be Jean's. The benzidine test indicated attempts to wipe clean blood from surfaces in the kitchen area. Patterns of blood spattering were consistent with a violent blow or blows to a portion of the human body and were inconsistent with a cut hand or similar injury. Tests indicated that the blood spatters were no more than two months old.

Dykshoorn felt that a young man came to the Larson home within 48 hours of the murder to help Clarence remove the body from the residence. The concealment of the body for removal from the residence could be easily accomplished with the attached garage situation. BCA agents and all other investigators involved in the case believed Jean was in all probability murdered and her body disposed of somewhere in Minnesota.

More than likely, Clarence never meant to kill his wife. An argument had gotten out of control, resulting in Jean's tragic death. It could very well have been an accident. The sad part is we may never know why Jean had to suffer such a tragic death, or where she is buried, but the search continues.

YEARS LATER

I ALWAYS WONDERED what happened to Clarence years later. What happened to his big house where he lived all alone? When was it sold? Where did Clarence end up living later in his life? I had to search for answers to these questions.

From people I spoke with, Clarence continued living in the big house all alone. He was shunned by most of the Tracy community but still managed to live a simple and peaceful life. He kept to himself most of the time.

While interviewing a family descendant, I found out that Clarence suffered from heart disease, and at some point, had heart surgery in Sioux Falls, South Dakota. Janet was with him at the time.

By 1994, Clarence was getting up in years. Living in the big house was more than he could handle on his own. He had closed off the big upstairs area and lived in a small portion of the main floor to conserve heat and electricity. He was eighty-four years old by now, living with chronic back pain along with his heart problems, when he decided it was time to sell the house. But since the house was owned in joint tenancy, and Jean had never been found, how could he legally declare sole ownership and full rights to the proceeds from the sale of the property? Clarence didn't let this deter him from his plan to sell the house and move to Tennessee to live with his daughter. He figured she would take care of him in his old age.

It was a very cold day in January 2018 when I headed out to the Lyon County courthouse, looking for answers. The drive from my residence to Marshall usually takes only about forty minutes, but once I backed out of my driveway, soft snowflakes began to fall, covering the highway, making the drive a bit treacherous. It took me an hour before I finally reached the courthouse parking lot. I turned the engine off but just sat there for several minutes, trying to compose myself after the long, scary drive, during which I almost slid off the road in a couple places along the way. I opened the car door and it slammed shut almost instantly. The wind was gusting something fierce and I traipsed around in the deep snow, looking for the entrance to the courthouse. I don't know why it took me so long to find the front door. Since I'd never been in this monstrous building before and was not sure where I should start searching or what I was looking for, I managed to get lost, walking through the many hallways and perusing all the names on the doors at every turn. I finally ended up on the second floor of the building in the assessor's office and met with Haylee, a woman who was kind enough to help me locate the deed on the Larson property. Below is what I discovered from looking through numerous records relating to this property.

I located documents which showed there was a hearing on October 28, 1994 in Fifth Judicial District, Probate Division at the courthouse in Lyon county. Clarence Larson appeared in person, along with his attorney, John D. Scholl of Worthington, Minnesota. Judge Marshall heard the "Findings of Fact" in the disappearance of Leona Jean Larson, aka Jean Larson. The court made the following Findings of Fact:

1. Absentee's name is Leona Jean Larson, aka Jean Larson
2. Date of birth is May 13, 1918
3. Last known address was 484 Craig Avenue, Tracy, Minnesota
4. Petitioner, Clarence L. Larson and absentee were married at the time absentee was last seen in October or November of 1980.
5. Absentee disappeared in October or November of 1980 and has been missing since that time.
6. Absentee has not been in communication with petitioner and he is not aware of anyone who has heard of, or heard from the absentee since the disappearance.
7. The Tracy Police and Lyon County Sheriff's office were involved in a search for the absentee.
8. Absentee's absence cannot be explained and has continued for more than four consecutive years.

9. Names and addresses of all known persons in interest are: Clarence Larson; Olivia Morris, daughter (aka Olivia Zoellner); Jennifer Sande, daughter; Charlotte Lief, guardian of Jennifer Sande.

The court makes its Conclusions of Law and Order:

1. The death of Leona Jean Larson, aka Jean Larson has been established as a matter of law.
2. Distribution of any property belonging to absentee should be distributed to above persons in the manner prescribed in Minnesota Statute Chapters 524 and 525.
3. The absentee's marriage to Clarence L. Larson is dissolved pursuant to Minnesota Statute 576.144.

The above Findings of Fact, Conclusions of Law and Order for Judgment, constitute the Judgment of the court on November 1, 1994, signed by George Marshall, Judge of District Court.

On June 5, 1995, the Office of County Recorder in Lyon county, filed the "Findings of Fact" which declared Leona Jean Larson, aka Jean Larson legally deceased and Clarence Larson was survivor and owner of Craig Avenue property. At this time, Jean's name was removed from the deed.

Now with sole ownership of the property, Clarence put the house up for sale. It wasn't long before a couple from the Tracy area made an offer on the house. The couple purchasing the property made the request that Jean's name be removed from the deed so there would be no demands on the property, if Jean should suddenly appear. Clarence made the remark to the prospective buyer, "And she would do that, too." But Clarence assured the couple that the title had been corrected. There weren't any further negotiations on the agreement, and the deal closed on July 19, 1995. It's likely Clarence took all the proceeds from the sale and fled to Tennessee, without giving any money to the other heirs of Jean's estate.

I was informed that on the day Clarence gave the keys to the new property owners, he had tears in his eyes; he just couldn't accept the fact he was leaving a home he had lived in for so many years. He slowly walked to the car, where his son was waiting. It was said that Clarence took the train to Tennessee to meet Janet. It was reported that Clarence and Janet lived together until she couldn't take care of him any longer. He was then placed in a nursing home nearby, where he died in 2002. His remains were transported to Minnesota, where he was buried next to Martha in the Zion Lutheran Cemetery near Balaton.

So, we wonder what happened to all the money Clarence accumulated after Martha's death. First of all, Clarence received $18,600 from the sale of the farm. Second, there was an undetermined amount received from the wrongful death suit, up to a maximum amount of $20,000. These two sources alone would have brought a substantial amount of money into his hands, which was a big chunk of money back then. What happened to all that money?

In Clarence's interviews with BCA agents, he mentioned that his "wife's drinking had cost him a considerable amount of money over the years." A large sum of money went toward Jean's hospitalization and other medical expenses. Clarence had major heart surgery, which was another big expense.

More money was spent when Clarence traveled to Omaha to visit his son on occasion, and many winters were spent in Tennessee with Janet.

In 1995, he sold the house, and at that time, Clarence was entitled to a widower's pension after Jean was declared dead, which would have been a substantial amount of money. He left Tracy with quite a bit of cash in his pocket. He spent the last few years of his life in Tennessee with Janet. Later on, some of that money probably went for his care at the nursing home. If there was any money left from his estate after he died, it probably went to Ron and Janet. For all of his ill-gotten gains, it was reported Clarence died a pauper.

THOSE LEFT BEHIND

RONALD LARSON WAS born July 15, 1938 in Tyler. He graduated in 1957 from Balaton High School in Balaton, Minnesota. He married Kolene Uhre in 1959 and they had four children; three boys and one girl. They later divorced. Then Ron married Linda Nitz on November 11, 1968 in Lakota, Iowa. They had two children, a son and a daughter. The couple lived in Omaha, Nebraska and later moved

Ron's graduation photo
Balaton year book 1957, from Balaton Area History Center

to McCook, Nebraska to be near the grandchildren. Ron worked as a carpenter and had his own company, R & L Construction. He enjoyed playing pool, fishing, shooting trap, woodworking, and visiting the grandchildren. He was a member of the McCook Eagles Club. He died on March 4, 2014 at the age of seventy-five. The memorial service was held on March 7 at the Carpenter Breland Funeral Chapel in McCook with Father Gary Brethour officiating. Interment was in the St. Patrick Calvary Cemetery in McCook.

Janet Larson was born August 12, 1943 in Slayton. She graduated in 1961 from Tracy High School. She attended the Stewart School in Sioux Falls, South Dakota for cosmetology. According to investigation records, she lived in Tennessee at the time of her father's death.

Olivia Sande was born June 30, 1946 in northern Minnesota. She graduated in 1964 from Tracy High School. From investigation records, we find out that her last name was "Zoellner" at the time of her mother's disappearance and she was living in Bozeman, Montana at the time.

To protect their privacy, I have not included any other information for Janet or Olivia.

LOST

A CRITICAL PART of any research into the past involves finding documents which verify the important events that make up the story. This is a very important task for any historian who wishes to resurrect a long-forgotten story. Of course, most of the search involves going through old newspapers and court documents. This is a huge undertaking. It's also a very exciting time for Debra and me as we search for pieces of past lives that make the story come alive.

Debra's expertise is in the area of genealogy. She spends many hours on Ancestry and other related sites searching for the early beginnings of the families in this story. Genealogy can be very confusing for me at times, but Debra does such an amazing job explaining how each family member is connected to the next, all the way down the line. From time to time, Debra travels to the MN History Center in St. Paul searching for information. She doesn't stop until she finds what she's looking for. We work as a team, gathering as much information as possible to report the story as accurately as we can.

It has now been almost fifty-nine years since Martha's tragic death and almost forty years since Jean's mysterious disappearance; so, one would expect most of the important documents relating to these two investigations would be long gone by this time, and that was certainly what happened during the course of our search. Many documents have been lost or destroyed. Below is a list of documents that were not found during our search.

Sheriff's Reports: In February 2020, I contacted Sheriff Steve Telkamp, Murray County Sheriff requesting the investigation file on Martha's suspicious death. He informed me that he'd have to do some checking and get back to me. I waited several weeks and contacted him again. The sheriff told me that all records from the 1960s had long since been destroyed, including the BCA's records of their investigation. I wasn't surprised, but instead, very disappointed.

Trial Transcript: I never located the court transcript of the murder trial. I must assume it has been destroyed. Court administrators in Murray, Cottonwood, and Lyon counties searched extensively for it for many months. It was not at the MN History Center either.

Death Certificate: I mailed the request for a copy of Clarence Larson's death certificate to Tennessee Department of Health in Nashville, Tennessee, but my request was returned. The reason given was that I was not directly related and not authorized to receive a copy.

<u>Contacts</u>: Another part of the research involves locating family members or friends who are still available and remember the facts in the case. This isn't always easy. Many of the people who knew about the Larsons are now deceased or memories have faded, so it's hard to find the missing pieces of the story. Sometimes people have moved out of the area and nobody knows where they are. Most people have cell phones, so you can't search for them with directory assistance. I've also posted comments on Facebook asking for help in locating family descendants. In December 2019, I placed an ad in the *Tracy Area Headlight Herald* asking people to share their stories about the Larson family, which resulted in a few good leads. Every new lead takes you down a new path of more intrigue and adventure; it's quite amazing the people you meet along the way.

FOUND

THE BEST PART of the search is finding things that you thought were long gone. Every bit of information found is like a precious gem; it's like going on an adventure to find the lost treasure. It's so very exciting for me when I make new discoveries that help tell the story. The feeling is indescribable; a most fascinating experience in my search for answers. Below is a list of documents discovered during the search.

Indictment Record: State of Minnesota vs. Clarence L. Larson, District Court, 6th Judicial District, County of Murray, State of Minnesota, dated December 4, 1962. Debra located this document at the MN History Center.

Coroner's Inquest Transcript: This important document took quite a bit of time to locate, but it was eventually found on microfilm at the Cottonwood County Courthouse in

Windom. I made an appointment to view the document. The court administrator had me sit in a small room, in front of the computer to read through 82 pages of witness testimony. I requested a copy; it arrived in a few weeks. This was one of the great discoveries in my search.

Birth Record: Clarence Ledu Larson was born April 23, 1910 in Scandia Township. His father, Charley Larson, was born in Iowa and his mother, Ida Anerhaug, was born in Norway.

Certificate of Death: Martha M. Larson died December 19, 1961; cause of death – skull fracture and brain damage, immediate; describe how injury occurred – unknown.

Wrongful Death Suit: State of Minnesota, County of Lyon, Clarence Larson vs. St. Paul Fire and Marine Insurance Company and National Fidelity Life Insurance Company, filed on May 10, 1963.

Box of Files: The box was located in the attic of the Tracy Police Station by Chief Jason Lichty. The box contained some of the investigation files regarding Jean Larson's disappearance. Included was the Missing Person Report received by Leon Van Den Broeke, Sheriff Lyon County; phone interview of Clarence Larson by officer Thomas Thompson; three search warrants by Lyon County Court; several interviews of people from Tracy conducted by the Bureau of Criminal Apprehension, Agents Berg and O'Gorman, and many other documents related to the investigation. The contents of this box was probably the most exciting discovery for me.

Imagine looking at evidence about a mysterious disappearance that no one has laid eyes on in close to forty years. As I read through the material, I became very emotional, feeling the seriousness of the situation, and at times, overwhelmed to tears, just wondering what happened to Jean. I also contacted Sheriff Eric Wallen, Lyon County Sheriff's office to review their file on the case. The file was massive—a stack of papers about 18" high. Most of the file contained the same information as what I saw in the Tracy file, but there were a few documents I hadn't seen before, which were included in the story.

Deed Documents: Deed Record No. 105, 103, 117, 122, 125; Warranty Deed 06779; Probate Court 20547, 247; Findings of Fact; Transfer of Title 0102736, and 0103536; relating to the Larson property.

CONCLUSION

IN REVIEWING MARTHA'S case, I wondered what led to her horrific death. It was most likely premeditated. I was curious to find out how much money Clarence received on the sale of his farm, so I contacted the Murray County Recorder's office. They looked up the deed; property was sold to Arvid Anderson on December 5, 1961 for $18,600; date recorded was January 8, 1962. Clarence took out a 31-day accident policy on Martha for $10,000 naming himself as beneficiary on December 8; eleven days later Martha died in a suspicious farm accident. This appeared to be the motive for murder. Clarence figured he'd collect $20,000 from the insurance companies and so he devised the scheme to get rid of Martha. It's possible Martha may have filed for divorce a few months before her death. Sheriff Neumann stated at the trial that he tried to serve legal papers on Clarence, but he was never home at the time. Could these legal papers have been related to a divorce filing? Martha would be entitled to half the proceeds on the sale of the farm as part of the divorce settlement. Clarence probably intended to keep all the money for himself.

For me, Martha's story is heartbreaking. Justice has never been served in her tragic death. Most everyone believed Clarence was guilty of murder and should have spent time in prison. If Clarence would have been locked up, Jean's terrible fate would have been avoided.

In reviewing Jean's case, investigators felt it was a homicide due to all the blood evidence found at the scene. There are still so many unanswered questions in this case. Remember what the psychic said, "her body would be found near water."

I recently received a call from a man who lives in Walnut Grove. He told me the following story. It was 1983, and he and his friend were in high school at the time. One day they were out walking along Plum Creek near Walnut Grove and they found some bones. They weren't sure if they were human bones. When they returned home, they told others of their discovery, and because people were still excited about the Larson case at the time, word spread throughout the community. Then a few days later, he and his friend were pulled out of class by BCA agents and other officials. The boys were asked to show them where they found the bones. They took them to the area where they thought the bones were discovered but weren't sure of the exact location. They searched around in the area, but the bones were never found. This story could be a possible link to where the psychic said Jean's remains would be found and where investigators had searched with grappling hooks in the Cottonwood River near Walnut Grove. Remember Clarence's fateful words, "Jean would surface again one day."

There's still no real justice or final answers regarding Jean's disappearance. I believe one day this case will be solved, so we can finally bring closure for Olivia. We need to know the truth of what happened to Jean.

Anyone who has information about Jean's disappearance should contact the Tracy Police Department at 507-629-5534 or the Lyon County Sheriff's office at 507-537-7666. You may remain anonymous. I believe if someone comes forward with reliable information, this case will be solved. Martha, Jean, and Clarence are all long gone, and it's time to hear the truth of what really happened to Martha and Jean. Someone out there has the answers, and I hope they will have the courage to come forward with the missing pieces of this story so we can bring closure for the Hatton, Stillings, and Larson family descendants.

REFERENCES

"2 Commit Suicide Within Three Days," Tracy Area Headlight Herald, November 16, 1950, pg. 1

"Currie Farmer Takes Own Life; Found Saturday Noon," Murray County Herald, November 16, 1950, pg. 1

"Fire Burns Barn Early Wednesday," Tracy Area Headlight Herald, June 9, 1955, pg. 1

"Power Takeoff Kills Farm Woman, 52," Tracy Area Headlight Herald, December 21, 1961, pg. 1

"Funeral for Mrs. Larson," Tracy Area Headlight Herald, December 28, 1961, pg. 6

"Lake Sarah farm woman killed by tractor PTO," Murray County Herald, December 1961, pg. 1

"Coroner's inquest held on farm woman's death," Murray County Herald, August 16, 1962, pg. 1

"Grand jury indicts spouse in death of farm woman," Murray County Herald, December 6, 1962, pg. 1

"Defense to ask court for change of venue in Larson murder trial," Murray County Herald, January 31, 1963, pg. 1

"Judge Flinn directs not guilty verdict in murder case," Murray County Herald, March 13, 1963

"Murder trial change of venue granted by court," Citizen and the Windom Reporter, February 7, 1963

"Murder trial starts Monday," Citizen and the Windom Reporter, February 28, 1963

"Jury Impaneled Tuesday Afternoon for Clarence Larson Murder Trial," Citizen and the Windom Reporter, March 6, 1963, pg. 1

"Larson trial begins," Citizen and the Windom Reporter, March 7, 1963

"Judge Grants "Not Guilty" Motion; Larson is Freed," Citizen and the Windom Reporter, March 13, 1963

"Murder Trial of Garvin Farmer to Start Second Week," Marshall Messenger, March 9, 1963

"Could Hear First Testimony Wednesday in Murder Trial," Mankato Free Press, March 5, 1963

"Six Testify at Murder Trial," Mankato Free Press, March 7, 1963

"State Attempts to Wrap up Case...," Mankato Free Press, March 8, 1963, pg. 7

"Acquittal in Windom Murder Trial," Mankato Free Press, March 13, 1963, pg. 8

Indictment Record, Murray County, Minnesota, 6th Judicial District Court, State of Minnesota against Clarence L. Larson, Murder in the First Degree on December 4, 1962, County Attorney J.T. Schueller

Inquest Testimonies of the death of Martha Larson before Coroner's Jury of the County of Murray, convened on August 14, 1962 and filed on September 10, 1962

Certificate of Death of Freeman Guy Pearsall, died November 9, 1950, age 56

Certificate of Death of Martha Larson, died December 19, 1961, age 52

Certificate of Death of Debra Jean Larson died July 5, 1965, age 4

"Police list Tracy woman as missing," Tracy Area Headlight Herald, November 13, 1980, pg. 1

"State agents seek clues in Tracy woman's disappearance," Tracy Area Headlight Herald, November 20, 1980, pg. 1

"No new leads in Tracy woman's disappearance," Tracy Area Headlight Herald, November 27, 1980, pg. 1

"Police search wide area for missing Tracy woman," Tracy Area Headlight Herald, pg. 1

"Police excavate property," Tracy Area Headlight Herald, December 18, 1980, pg. 1

"Searching Shetek area for clues," Tracy Area Headlight Herald, January 22, 1981, pg. 3

"Tracy missing person case still active," Tracy Area Headlight Herald, March 26, 1981, pg. 1

"Psychic consultant enters Larson case," Tracy Area Headlight Herald, April 23, 1981, pg. 1

"Investigation continues," Tracy Area Headlight Herald, April 30, 1981, pg. 1

"Sheriff's office reminds residents of reward offer," Tracy Area Headlight Herald, July 2, 1981, pg. 2

Box of documents including -- Missing person report, Lyon County Sheriff's Department, three search warrants, BCA Investigative Reports and interviews of neighbors and friends. Permission to review files by Jason Lichty, Chief of Police. Permission to review Lyon County Sheriff's office files by Sheriff Eric Wallen.

Complaint -- State of Minnesota, County of Lyon, Clarence Larson vs. St. Paul Fire and Marine Insurance Company and National Fidelity Life Insurance Company, filed on May 10, 1963.

Deed Documents – Deed Record No. 105, 103, 117, 122, 125; Warranty Deed 06779; Probate Court 20547, 247; Findings of Fact; Transfer of Title 0102736, 0103536 relating to the Larson property.

ACKNOWLEDGEMENTS

THE RESEARCH FOR this project was extensive, taking several years to compile. I met so many amazing people along the way that helped tell this story. Many people provided personal stories, pertinent information and details about this case. I discovered so many missing pieces to this story, but there are still many pieces yet to be found.

There are many people to thank for assisting me in bringing this story to life. First, I must give a special thank you to Debra Gangelhoff, my dear friend and research specialist, who does such an amazing job digging up lost information in old newspapers, court documents, history books or other archival material. She also critiques the manuscript. I can't thank her enough for all she does for me.

The research for this book included contacting court administrators, Murray County and Lyon County Sheriffs' offices, the Minnesota Bureau of Criminal Apprehension, the Tracy Police Department, and the Tracy Area Headlight Herald newspaper office.

Much gratitude is given to the following people for their dedication to this project – Denise Brandel, Kim Jelen, Sheila Pierson, court administrators; LuAnn Fier, Haylee Jensen, recorder's office; Jason Lichty, Tracy Chief of Police; Eric Wallen, Lyon County Sheriff; Per Peterson, and Lisa Sell, Tracy Area Headlight Herald.

A big thank you to those dedicated people who preserve history at the following museums – Balaton Area History Center, Janet Timmerman, Murray County Museum; Jan Louwagie, Southwest State University Library; Jon Wendorff, Wheels Across the Prairie Museum, and Chris True, Minnesota History Center. They were very helpful in providing information and photos.

Special thank you to my copy editor, Joan Rogers, who always does such a wonderful job editing the manuscript, and to all the staff at Outskirts Press who help me get through the publishing process.

When I first started out on this adventure, I didn't quite know what to expect. I was a bit leery there wouldn't be anyone around that remembered Clarence Larson or even wanted to talk to me about what happened to Martha and Jean all those years ago, but I was pleasantly surprised to find out that so many people were excited to hear I was documenting this story. For me, this story was an emotional journey into the past, but it was important to find the truth of what happened to Martha and Jean. There were many stories of Clarence over the years that turned out to be nothing but rumors and hearsay so I made it my mission to report the facts, if I could.

I want to extend a special thank you to the following people who shared their memorable stories of Clarence, Martha and Jean. I am forever grateful to them – Rueben and Jeane Anderson, Wayne Brock, John DeBlieck, Lee DeBlieck, Diane Deming, Ken Gleason, Kurt Halverson, Doris Hemish, Dean Larson, Kathy Phillips, Jeff Lee, Raymond Marsh, Mike and Rosemary Martin, Mary Mattson, Fred Menger, Dan Peterson, Rolana Schmidt, and Larry Sloan.

ABOUT THE AUTHOR

PATRICIA LUBECK IS from Echo, a small town in southwestern Minnesota. She graduated from Echo High School, attended the University of Minnesota, and eventually made her home in California where she earned her Bachelor of Arts Degree from the University of California. Years later, she returned to Minnesota, accepting the position of director at the Yellow Medicine County museum. It was here where she became interested in the local history, researching early crimes in the area. While reading old newspapers, she was inspired to bring these long-forgotten stories back to life. Her first book was published in 2012; a story about the only man who was executed in Redwood County in 1891. Her other books are collections of short stories including various types of murder, mystery, and mayhem in Redwood, Renville and Yellow Medicine counties. This is her fifth book. Anyone who loves reading true crime stories and has a passion for history, will enjoy her books. They are available at Outskirts Press, Amazon and Barnes and Noble.

www.outskirtspress.com/VictimsofFoulPlay

Murder in Gales, A Rose Hanged Twice
Murder, Mystery and Mayhem in Minnesota
Crime and Calamity in Yellow Medicine County
Murder and Madness

CPSIA information can be obtained
at www.ICGtesting.com
Printed in the USA
LVHW051629131220
674080LV00042B/2280